M. E. M'Allister

Sunshine among the Clouds

Extracts from Experience

M. E. M'Allister

Sunshine among the Clouds
Extracts from Experience

ISBN/EAN: 9783337341053

Printed in Europe, USA, Canada, Australia, Japan

Cover: Foto ©Thomas Meinert / pixelio.de

More available books at **www.hansebooks.com**

Sunshine Among the Clouds:

OR,

Extracts from Experience.

BY

MRS. M. E. M'ALLISTER.

With an Introduction by Rev. G. B. Jocelyn, D. D.

"*My experience is not my own: God has given it, and I am not at liberty to withhold it.*"

CINCINNATI:
HITCHCOCK AND WALDEN.
FOR THE AUTHOR.
1873.

Entered, according to Act of Congress, in the year 1873,

BY MRS. M. E. M'ALLISTER,

In the Office of the Librarian of Congress, at Washington.

TO

The Loved Ones in Christ,

WHO HAVE BEEN THE COMPANIONS AND HELPERS IN FAITH DURING THE CONFLICTS, AND PARTAKERS OF THE TRIUMPHS, NARRATED IN THESE PAGES;

AND ESPECIALLY

TO THOSE WHO MOURN FOR THE "GONE FROM EARTH,"

OF WHOM THESE IMPERFECT REMEMBRANCES ARE GIVEN,

This Little Book

IS AFFECTIONATELY DEDICATED BY

THE AUTHOR.

PREFACE.

THE contents of the first eight chapters of this unpretending volume were collected from scattered papers, with no intention of publication, at a time when I supposed that earth's pilgrimage was nearly ended.

The motive prompting to this was, that the experiences as therein narrated would be a comfort to my dear parents, husband, and children, when I should be resting with the redeemed.

With returning health came the conviction that these experiences might be made a blessing to others, and that I had no right to withhold them; nor could I find rest of mind until in my closet I promised God that I would place the same in the hands of those considered competent judges, and that thus the voice of the Church should be to me the voice of God.

This was done, and the decision made to publish; but in this I seemed strangely prevented, from time to time, until since the experience as narrated in the last two chapters.

Cautious and shrinking nature strongly pleaded that these experiences be withheld; while, on the other hand, the influence of God's providence and Spirit seem urging to give them.

Believing that His own hand leadeth me, I cast them as bread upon the waters, expecting that, in the day of the solving of life's mystery, I shall know of the whys and wherefores.

I only give these unusual manifestations in dreams, etc., because they have been to me messengers of comfort and joy; and while I would lay little stress upon them—knowing that God's revealed Word is the true and all-sufficient lamp for our feet—I have been led to accept them as way-marks in the path of glory, and through them to trust the more fully in Him who so tenderly leads his children through their own darkness into his light.

THE AUTHOR.

CONTENTS.

INTRODUCTION, ... PAGE 13

CHAPTER I.

Our Commission—Blessings of Childhood—Early Conversion—Wanderings of Heart—Convictions of the Necessity of Holiness—Years of Seeking—The Rest of Faith gained—Conflicts and Victories in regard to Profession—Witness of the Spirit lost—Witness of the Spirit regained—Blessedness of the Life of Faith—Remembrances of Former Teachings of the Spirit—The Land of Beulah no longer in the Distance—Why Christians complain of Darkness—The Earth between them and Christ—Longings for Closer Communion with God—Answer to Prayer realized—The trial of Faith—Glorious Deliverance from Temptation, ... 19

CHAPTER II.

At Quincy Camp-meeting—Victories of the Cross over Natural Timidity—Work for All—The Insufficiency of Earthly Honors or Emulations to attract the Soul—The Sting of Death removed—Triumphant Death of Mother Page—Interest in

Bible-class—Bible-class Prayer-meeting—The Want of More Holy Members in the Church—Contending with the Powers of Darkness—The Eternal Word a Strong Tower—Earnest Desires to be More Christ-like—Lessons in the Way of Faith—Consciousness of being brought Nearer Christ—The Darkness and Sorrow brought by the Bloodshed in the Land—Enlistment of Companion in the Service of his Country—Motives Influencing—Power of Prayer to calm the Soul—The Parting—Assurances of meeting again—The Safety and Joyousness of the Narrow Way—Again at Quincy Camp-meeting—The Strength given in "The Just shall live by Faith"—Comfort in a Night Vision, PAGE 41

CHAPTER III.

Suffering of Mind in regard to Companion—Dream of attending his Funeral—Wonderful Blessing in the lifting above Earthly Things of May 11th—A Special Prayer, and Assurance gained—The Much-feared Cup of Sorrow given to drink—The Anguish hidden in the Few Words, "Mortally wounded on the Eleventh"—Great Triumph in Death—Messages of Comfort—Funeral Services—Glimpses of the Light on the Other Shore—Further Intelligence from Richmond—The Dying Message—Darkness of National Affairs—The Refuge of the Christian—Blessings of Christian Sympathy—Heart-searchings before God—The Witness of the Spirit Dimmed—Desire to know that all FELT meets the Divine Approval—Blessings of the Sanctuary—The "Star of Promise"—Full Particulars of Death of Husband—Answer of the Prayer of May 11th—Belief in a Special Providence strengthened—A Richmond Hospital made Light—The Stability of Jerusalem Above—Brighter Stars than those of Earthly Conquerors gained—Sorrow of the Land turned to Rejoicing—Tears of Widows and Orphans bottled in Heaven—Victory over Suffering, and Nearness to the Heavenly Jerusalem—Rest of Soul regained—Definite Testimony—Walking in the Light—The Trial and Victory, ... 54

CHAPTER IV.

Christian Communion—Chosen in the Furnace of Affliction—Earthly Good relinquished for Treasure in Heaven—A Remembrance of Mrs. C. E. M'Allister—Among Strangers—Filled with "Joy Unspeakable and Full of Glory"—New Year commenced—Labor at F.—Quarterly-meeting—An Incident of the Meeting—Re-echoings of "Tell my Family to meet me in Heaven"—Presence of the Lord with his People—Decisions for Eternity—A Realization of "All Things work together for Good," etc.—Sufferings of Earth bringing Nearer to Christ—Not a Separated Family—The Christian's Legacy, ... PAGE 76

CHAPTER V.

Incompetency of Earthly Powers to tell the Joys of the Redeemed—Albion Centenary Camp-meeting—Thoughts of the Past, Present, and Future—Christian Fellowship—Struggle of Soul, and Victory gained by Faith—Heavenly Places—A Realization of the "Victory gained by Faith"—Gift of Power received—Anticipations of the Future Fellowship of Souls made One in Christ—Binding of the Offering upon the Altar—Ann Arbor Camp-meeting—Overpowering Manifestation of the Divine Presence—Meeting with Dr. and Mrs. Palmer—Victories of the Cross—The Banner of Holiness—He set a Child in the Midst of Them, ... 95

CHAPTER VI.

Prepared—A Remembrance of Miss M. L. Smith—Unprepared—Moscow Camp-meeting—New Conference Year commenced—Discouragements—The Foundation of God's Word a Firm Rock—Answer to Prayer in Eddy's Mission, . . 114

CHAPTER VII.

Remembrance of Rev. H. Law—The Broken Vow, and Remorse of Conscience in Death—A Realization of the Promise, "In All thy Ways acknowledge Him, and He shall direct thy Paths"—Unexpected Trial—Prevailing Prayer—Burden of Soul for Unconverted, and Deep Convictions of the Unsaved—Specific Prayer—Power of Faith, ... PAGE 126

CHAPTER VIII.

Remembrance of Rev. J. Jennings—His Religious Experience—A Visit to his Sick-room—Dying Utterances—Renewal of Christian Associations on Coldwater Camp-ground—Vacant Places—Strengthened to contend for Scriptural Holiness—Memorable Evening—White Raiment—Albion Feast of Tabernacles—Light about the River—Desire to live and labor—New Witnesses—Annual Conference—Morning Love-feast—Zion arising—Mrs. H. Brockway—Mrs. E. Crane—Her Character and Experience as described by a Friend—Christmas-gift—Soul Aspirations—Joyful Anticipation of the Future, . . . 144

CHAPTER IX.

Remembrance of Rev. E. Crane—Suffering, instead of doing, the Will of God—Suggestions of Adversary—Victory gained at Family Altar—Preserved Blameless—Conference at Three Rivers—Bishop Ames's Remarks upon the Inner Life—Eternity none too long for the Revealing of the Mystery—Remembrance of Brucie Hoag—"He shall SIT as a Refiner," etc.—Sympathy with Christ the Christian's Power—Remembrance of Willie Daugherty—Blessedness of Life—Influence—Key-stone of the Arch, ... 163

CHAPTER X.

Moscow—Our Welcome at the Parsonage—Expecting the Harvest—Failure of the Health of Mr. M'Allister—A Treasure—Conversion of Allie—New Experience regarding Public Work—Entering of Woman's Foreign Missionary Work—First Appointment—Experience at Albion Camp-meeting—License Question agitated—Perplexity of Mind—Experience at the Close of Meeting—Awake in the Night with the Words, "Go ye"—Doubts regarding Duty—Decision to go forward—License Question again hinders—North Adams—Labor at Union City—Decision to avoid Every Thing that looks in the Direction of *Special* Public Work—Anticipation of Mr. M'Allister regarding Regular Work—Gains Some Victory—Speedy Answer to a Special Request—At Hanover—Illness of Mr. M'Allister—Sent of the Lord—Disappointment—Application of "I was brought low, and He helped me"—Experience at Bedside of Companion—View of the River of Death—Expectation of Recovery—New Conflicts and Difficulties—Letter from Mrs. M. L. Crawford—Struggle and Victory—Conversation with Pastor—Cross lifted—Victory—Improving Health of Companion—Anticipated United Labor for Christ—Suddenly taken Worse—Hope departing—Strengthened by the coming of Mrs. M. L. Jordan, . PAGE 186

CHAPTER XI.

Triumphant Death-bed Scene of Rev. J. E. M'Allister—Conflict with Adversary—Mrs. M. L. Crawford awakened by a Voice saying, "Your Precious Friend's Husband is Dead"—Opening of Way for Public Work—Divine Strength imparted—Labors at Home—License to Exhort given—Examination passed for License to Preach—Prejudices and Self-will at the Feet of Jesus—Severe Conflict and Victory—St. Joseph—Benton Harbor—Items in the Experience of Mrs. M. L. Crawford—Experience of Full

Salvation—View of the Cross—Special Prayer brings Special Blessing—Hears Angelic Choristers—Return Home—Comforted by the Reflection of Earth Lights—Anticipation of the "Welcome Home" on the Other Shore, .   .   .   **PAGE 212**

INTRODUCTION.

THE narration of Christian experience is one of the means which God uses to comfort his children and advance the interests of his kingdom. As he has promised that we shall not be tempted above that which we are able to bear, the experience of others becomes a demonstration to us that the promises of God will be fulfilled.

The feeling of dependence is so strong in us, that we not only lean upon God, but upon each other, for support. This is most strikingly manifest in all matters pertaining to our spiritual life. God seems to have so ordered it that his Word and his Spirit lead us to himself through our fellows, as instruments. Occasionally, his Spirit may convict and convert a soul without the intervention of a fellow-spirit, but the instances are rare. In matters of salvation, we are "workers together with God." By us the Word is preached; by us witness is borne to all around, that the "Son of Man hath power on earth not only to forgive sins, but to cleanse from all unrighteousness;" by us the life of faith—the "life hid with Christ in God"—is to be so lived that we are to represent him, and, in "his stead, beseech men to be reconciled to God."

An angel of God may appear unto the devout Cornelius, and say: "Thy prayers and thine alms are come up for a memorial before God;" but he attempts not to preach the Gospel, but adds: "Send men to Joppa and call for Simon, whose surname is Peter: . . . he shall tell thee what thou oughtest to do." Peter is instructed by a vision with reference to the said Cornelius; but it was not until he told the story of the Cross, and announced himself as a witness that "remission of sins" is through faith in the name of Christ, that the Holy Ghost fell upon Cornelius and those that were with him, as upon the apostles on the day of Pentecost. Why did not the angel preach Jesus to Cornelius?

The persecuting and blood-stained Saul of Tarsus may be stricken to the earth on his road to Damascus, and see and converse with the risen and ascended Savior, but in reply to the question, "Lord, what wilt thou have me to do?" he does not receive a direct answer, but is told, "Arise, and go into the city, and it shall be told thee what thou must do." And it is not until after three days of darkness and fasting and prayer, when the Divinely instructed Ananias enters the house where he is, "and putting his hands on him, said, Brother Saul, the Lord, even Jesus, that appeared unto thee in the way as thou camest, hath sent me that thou mightest receive thy sight and be filled with the Holy Ghost," that he received sight, was baptized, and began to "preach that Jesus is the Son of God." Why was not Paul converted at the time he so humbly asked, "What wilt thou have me to do?"

As it was then, so it is now. Few, if any, are converted or sanctified, only as they come in contact with the experience of others who enjoy these blessings.

The apostles, in obedience to a specific command, remained in Jerusalem until they received the gift of the Holy Ghost, that they might be "witnesses unto Christ;" and when they were filled with the Holy Ghost, they spake as the Spirit gave them utterance, and preached remission of sins and the gift of the Holy Spirit unto every one who repented and called upon the name of the Lord; and multitudes were added unto their number, and witnessed to a present and full salvation in the name of Jesus.

All along the ages, the relation of personal experience has been an element of power in the Christian Church. "I am a Christian," was the utterance of the martyrs; and, despite the fagot and the stake and the block, the witnesses for Jesus were multiplied.

In the days of early Methodism in this land, the apostolic custom of "telling one's experience" was followed by the ministers, and many were led to the Savior. The class-meeting and love-feast have been the instruments of the conversion of hundreds of thousands; and it will be a sad day for Methodism when these places for the relation of Christian experience are not attended by the masses of the Church, and when ministers forget to tell how and when they were released from the guilt and dominion of sin.

Frequently the pen supplies, in a measure, the place of the tongue, and letters and books are made the medium by which Christian experience is narrated to the honor and glory of God. Books of personal experience have many disadvantages, and, on the whole, are not equal to oral testimony, yet they have some advantages. Books can be with you and speak when the nearest and dearest personal friends can not. Over the written or printed pages you can linger and meditate and pray; and, as you drink in the spirit of the writer, the Holy Spirit enlightens your mind and leads you to that fountain where all sin and uncleanness are washed away. Many souls have been awakened by the tract and the written Word; many have been led to seek a fuller baptism of the Spirit by reading the experience of men and women eminent for their spirituality, and seeing in that experience a practical application of the promises of God to them in answer to their prayer and faith.

One want of the Church, at the present time, is clear, well-written narrations of Christian experience, covering the whole life of faith. We have many books of precepts, of doctrine, of controversy. These are necessary, and are accomplishing their work. Something more is needed. Books illustrating the power of the grace of God in daily life are needed by the Church, and these illustrations must be drawn from real life, and name and date and place given. Illustrations, such as are frequently given in the garb of fiction, however true to nature they may be, will not do. The soul longs to hear some other souls tell by pen or tongue what God has done for them; and, when such souls speak, the fainting heart is revived, the doubting heart believes, and the hungry and thirsty heart is filled. May God multiply books of Christian experience!

This little book is such a work. It is a plain account of the dealings of God with one of his children, in the ordinary walks of life. The greater portion of the work is in the form of a diary, and the daily blessings and trials, temptations and victories, are enumerated. It is the experience of one who has been made a partaker of the blessings of perfect love, and who feels that it is her duty to tell the riches of grace in Christ Jesus to her, that others may be emboldened to step into that "higher life," and thus be qualified to labor more efficiently for God. Her simple narration will do good to all who may read it. If they are seeking for holiness of heart, it will aid them; if they enjoy it, it will stimulate them to renewed zeal, a more open confession of Christ, and a more careful illustration in their lives of a state of grace ignored by some, misapprehended by many, and misrepresented by others. May God, who "is able to do exceeding abundantly above all that we ask or think," make these pages a blessing to thousands!

G. B. J.

Albion College.

SUNSHINE AMONG THE CLOUDS.

CHAPTER I.

OUR COMMISSION.

IT was an hour of darkness and gloom to the little band of disciples. He on whom they had looked as Israel's Redeemer, had been crucified, and his body was now lying in the tomb.

> "Ah! death seemed all-conquering when he bound
> The Lord of Life in prison!"

But, "As it began to dawn"—fit emblem of a more glorious light dawning upon our sin-cursed world than mortal saw—"came Mary Magdalene and the other Mary, to see the sepulcher. And, behold, there was a great earthquake: for the angel of the Lord descended from heaven, and came and rolled back the stone from the door, and sat upon it. His countenance was like lightning, and his raiment white as snow. And for fear of him the keepers did shake, and became as dead men. And the angel answered and said unto the women, Fear not ye: for I know that ye seek Jesus, which was crucified. He is not here: for he has risen, as he said. Come, see the place where the Lord lay. And go quickly, and tell his disciples that he is risen from the dead." What a change!

> "The might of death was nowhere found,
> When Christ again was risen."

Marys of the present age! Have we seen the light shining in a dark place? Has the day dawned? the day-star arisen in our hearts? Has the light, seen afar down through the vista of ages yet to come, brightening with glowing ray the pages of an Isaiah, giving beauty to the prophesies of a weeping Jeremiah, entered our soul?

> "How blessed are our eyes
> That see this heavenly light!
> Prophets and kings desired it long,
> But died without the sight."

But hear our commission! *"Go quickly and tell his disciples* that he is risen from the dead!" Not, let thy lips be sealed while the soul burns within for joy thereof; but hasten, while the sepulcher's open, the breezes blowing from Calvary's mountain; while He liveth to make intercession for the sins of the people, to redeem from all iniquity, and sanctify unto himself a peculiar people; while by blessed experience thou art proving that Christ is a risen Savior, that his blood cleanseth, washeth whiter than snow,—*go, bear the glad news!* PUBLISH IT! The Master saith: "Be not afraid. My presence shall go with thee, and I will give thee rest."

Tell the Church her bridal attire awaiteth her; the promise of the Father *is* hers. Tell that group mourning over the desolations of Zion, in gloom singing of former days of gladness, but making no effort to rebuild her walls, to arise and shine, for their light *is* come.

Tell those mourning ones, weeping above newly made graves, that Jesus hath passed through the tomb, broken its bars, and now glory gilds the grave, paving the way to heaven.

O, blessed privilege—with so glorious a light shining above, beneath, and all around us, to go forth amid the gloom of a world lying in wickedness, telling to all, from the king upon his throne to the beggar at the rich man's gate, the joyful news of a risen Redeemer!

Such a life, though it be one of comparative obscurity, leaves ever beside its pathway, *immortal* monuments. The world may not discern them; they, seeing so dimly through the mists and vapors of sin, perceive nought but those that are tinged with gold, and rear proudly toward heaven. *These shall crumble into dust;* but a life of faith that goeth forth, bearing precious seed, with its record on high, shall not die, but live forever; and though it be but the giving of the "cup of cold water" in the name of a disciple, *immortality* is stamped upon it.

Years have passed since in this we saw our commission. We looked upon the great harvest-field, with earnest longings upon the work of those who, scattering broadcast over our land the seeds of Scriptural holiness, were already reaping an abundant harvest; then upon our own unfitness for a work so important,—and our heart sank within us. Then we read the encouraging words: "*Ruth gleaned in the fields of Boaz.*"

"If you can not in the harvest
Gather up the richest sheaves,
Many a grain both ripe and golden,
Will the careless reapers leave.

Go and glean among the briers
Growing rank against the wall;
For it may be that their shadow
Hides the heaviest wheat of all."

We saw our work; and, though never able to point to splendid services in the cause of our Master, though not ours to wield the sickle in the ripened field, we do expect when, with the redeemed millions we shout the harvest-home, to be able, all of grace, to carry our sheaves with us.

> "Happy then will be those *gleaners*
> Who have sheaves to carry home."

Amid our gleanings, these Christian experiences have been gathered, and, trusting that to some traveler with us to the better country, they may prove as would a "cup of cold water given in the name of a disciple," we give them.

December 1, 1858. The past of my life has been bountifully strewn with the blessings of a kind heavenly Father. Very early in life the seeds were sown in my heart by Christian parents, which ought to produce the hundred-fold; and God be praised that the lessons of early childhood have not been upon altogether unfruitful soil! The seed has germinated. O, that it may finally become as "the tree planted by the rivers of water, that bringeth forth his fruit in his season; his leaf also shall not wither, and whatsoever he doeth shall prosper!"

When not yet nine years of age, I bowed with my parents at the altar of prayer, a weeping penitent, feeling keenly my need of a Savior, and arose happy in the consciousness of sins forgiven. The joy of that hour, though fourteen years have since passed, is still fresh in my memory.

It was but the conversion of *a child*, 't is true; but angels in heaven struck anew their golden harps, and the song in which the millions around the throne joined was over a child saved from the power and dominion of sin. My conversion I have never doubted. My evidence was as clear as the midday sun. The next morning, on awakening, I took up the family Bible—"which lay on the stand"—and opened to these words: "O Lord, I will praise thee: for though thou wast angry with me, thine anger is turned away, and thou comfortest me;" and for some time praise was continually upon my tongue. God be praised that children may know on earth their sins forgiven, and retain that evidence too! O, for more fathers and mothers in Israel to lead forward to green pastures these tender lambs of the fold!

For some years I was faithful; then, as the temptations of youth clustered around me, my experience relapsed into that of thousands at the present day:

"Now I repent; now sin again;
Now I revive, and now am slain."

That there was for the Christian a nobler, higher, and holier experience, I knew; for from childhood I had been surrounded by living witnesses of the power of grace to save *even unto the uttermost:* and through the influence of these, and the reading of such books as Mrs. Fletcher, Hester A. Rogers, Mrs. Palmer, and others, I was led to see the beauty and excellency of a life of holiness in contrast with my own; and the necessity of purity of heart as a preparation for a life of usefulness, and the abundant entrance to that city to which nothing unholy or unclean ever gains admittance, became, as never before, a reality, until

"My restless soul cried out, oppress'd,
 Impatient to be freed."

Yet, not discerning the simple way of faith, trusting to a degree in my own works, deeming that in order to claim the blessing a certain summit of feeling must be attained, it would at times seem that I but wept, fasted, and prayed in vain.

"O, how many a glorious record had the angels of me kept,
 Had I done instead of doubted, had I warred instead of wept!"

At other seasons, the blessing seemed just within my reach. Then I would start back as some cross would be presented, proving the depth of meaning in the interrogation: "How can ye believe which receive honor one of another and seek not the honor that cometh from God only?"

O, the groans, the tears, the fastings of those

years in which my soul refused to submit fully to Christ! How fully have they proved to this heart that

> "No outward form can make us clean;
> The leprosy lies deep within!"

A year ago last September, my wearied soul exclaimed, "I can not, nor *will* I, longer rest until pure within;" and alone in my room I bowed, resolved to count the cost *then* and *there*, let the sacrifice be what it might. O, how ready is the Spirit of God to lead us, when we submit to be led! I had but just commenced the struggle, crying, "Now, Lord, give me the blessing now!" when a voice seemed to whisper to my soul, hushing it to quietness, "This struggling is not necessary;" then the words, "Likewise reckon ye also yourselves to be dead indeed unto sin, but alive unto God through Jesus Christ our Lord." Very clearly was presented to my mind, through the light of the Spirit shining upon the written Word, the terms, "*Wherefore come out from among them and be ye separate*, saith the Lord, and touch not the unclean thing;" and the promise, "*I* WILL RECEIVE *you*," accompanied by the precious exhortation: "Having, therefore, these promises, dearly beloved, *let us cleanse ourselves from all filthiness of the flesh and spirit*, perfecting holiness in the fear of God." The consecration in the light given was made—time, talent, influence; and O, how these now appeared as not my own!—and the dearest idols I had were all laid upon the altar, and I arose with no other change of feeling than that of the consciousness of having met the Divine requirement, and a quiet sinking out of self into the will of God.

I had expected some wonderful manifestation, an overwhelming joy; and here was only the feeling of one long tossed upon the billows at the mercy of the waves, now anchored in the harbor of repose, a consciousness of safety, of security inexpressible, and a fear of moving lest it should be from my hiding-place in the clefts of the Rock.

But not an hour had passed before it was suggested to my mind, You will have to tell this to your companion (who was then absent from home). This was the first cross. But remembering that by virtue of my consecration I was no longer my own, I immediately took my pen and wrote of the consecration made, adding the expression of my faith in the blood that cleanseth from all sin. The moment this was done, my soul was filled to overflowing. The Spirit, bearing witness with mine, came, and laying down my pen, I long gave vent to the joy within in shouts of praise.

But a short time passed before again was

presented to my mind the duty of bearing direct testimony before the Church, both in the public social circles and in private conversation, of the grace received. The tempter suggested: "Better wait and let the fruit speak for itself. You are in a land of strangers, and know of no one in this crowded city Church who professes to have present personal knowledge of the efficacy of the blood of Christ to cleanse from all sin. Would not definite testimony upon your part savor of pride?"

Sabbath morning came, and I repaired to my class-room. Testimonies were given, but nothing was said by either leader or class-mates of "*holiness.*" O, how I longed to there find some soul beating in sympathy with mine! But I found it not. I arose to my feet, thinking, "I'll speak clearly of the consecration made, but will be careful of expressions, so as not to give to my brethren and sisters cause for offense;" but had no sooner began telling of the past years of wandering in the wilderness, the longings after more of the inner-life, holiness of heart, and of the consecration made during the past week, than the blessing of God came upon me, causing a hitherto unknown boldness, and, instead of saying as intended, "I think the offering is accepted," I said, "I KNOW the offering is accepted, and the *blood of Christ* CLEANSETH." But I had no sooner taken my seat than the adversary met me, and accused me of boasting; and then, that I was myself deceived and was deceiving others. In this state of mind I went into the audience-room, and so great became the conflict in my own mind that nothing of the sermon was heard, and I returned to my home in an agony of mind seemingly unendurable, resolved alone with my God to settle the question; and again, in the secret place, I threw myself upon the *Immutable Word*, and found my feet again pressing solid rock. To God be all the glory, who knoweth how to deliver from temptation, and who causeth the trial of our faith to be " more precious than of gold that perisheth."

For some months I was enabled to hold fast my confidence in the direct testimony of the Spirit relative to the grace received. Moral power was given, and O how sweet to labor in the vineyard of the Master, while I testified to the Church and a wondering world, " Great peace have they which love thy law, and nothing shall offend them!" But the All-wise Father saw my need of different discipline. Cares multiplied. Ill health deprived me of the means of grace in which my soul so much delighted; and, by degrees, the witness of the Spirit became unnecessarily dim. The knowledge of the present application of the blood of Christ to cleanse from all impurity, declined into the question, "Does it now cleanse me?"

But who that has fed in green pastures can be content upon the barren mountain of unbelief? Again, last December 14th, in my extremity I cried:

> "Only thou, my leader be,
> And I still will follow thee."

Then I remembered it is written, "If we WALK in the light, as He IS in the light, we have fellowship one with another, and the blood of Jesus Christ his Son *cleanseth us from all sin.*" I saw no way of retreat, nor did I desire it. The cry of my longing heart was:

> "Nearer, my God, to thee!
> Nearer to thee!
> E'en though it be a cross
> That raiseth me."

The answer came. The voice I knew. It was that of the Comforter—"I have come and brought the Father with me"—while a voice of reproof for former unbelief, yet of such tender compassion that my soul melted before it, said, "Reach hither thy finger and behold my hands; and reach hither thy hand and thrust it into my side, and be not faithless, but believing." Quickly my soul responded, "Henceforth, when the joys of sense depart, I will walk by faith alone." O, how precious to my soul the answer of my merciful High Priest, "Then God shall be glorified ; Christ magnified." The blessedness of that hour's communion is still with me.

"My flesh which cries, 'It can not be,'
Shall silence keep before the Lord."

Mine is the joy of knowing that all I have or am, or ever expect to be, is given to Christ. "Behold, we have forsaken all and followed thee. What shall we have therefore?" "In the world ye shall have tribulation; but be of good cheer: I have overcome the world."

My legacy I have read. It's the will of the Unchangeable: "Whether Paul, or Apollos, or Cephas, or the world, or life; or death, or things present, or things to come: ALL *are mine:* and I am Christ's: and Christ is God's." Unto him will I go, without the camp, bearing his reproach until it is said, "It is enough: Child, come home!" Then gladly shall I drop this tenement of clay, and, clad in immortality, join the redeemed - above.

January 6, 1859. The last moments of the Old Year were spent in renewed consecration of all to Christ. The adversary of late has ceased his endeavors to make me believe that I am not wholly the Lord's. Perfect faith puts doubt to flight.

Through the grace of God I am enabled to testify that, " The life which I now live in the flesh I live by the faith of the Son of God, who loved me and gave himself for me." O, blessed consciousness of Divine favor! O, the blessedness of hearkening to the commands of the unseen! My peace is as a river. Twice, of late, while worshiping with the people of God, I have been filled with joy unspeakable and full of glory, and had I held my peace, the very stones must have cried out. " Cry out and shout, thou inhabitant of Zion; for great is the Holy One of Israel in the midst of thee."

January 7th. A cold, windy, and stormy night. All without seems in commotion ; but in my heart there is a sweet peace given by Him who of old spoke to the troubled deep, " Peace, be still !" I look back with wonder upon the long years in which my soul has been so tempest-tossed, seeking rest and quietness. Why, O why, did I not cast my anchor within the veil, and let it take hold upon Christ?

> " O'er life's rough ocean wave
>   Fast was I going ;
> By threat'ning tempests driven, and billows tost.
>   And surges deep of woe,
>   My soul o'erflowing !
> O, all seem'd lost without Thee—lost, all lost."

But now,
> "My faith hath caught the gaze—
> I now behold Thee:
> And now let tempests wing their chilling frost;
> Thy mildly melting ray
> Beams sweetly o'er me—
> But without Thee, I am lost—in darkness lost."

Just now I am reminded of an experience of several years ago. Was visiting in company with a friend at the home of a dear sister, who had long been walking the narrow way, and in my night-visions seemed recounting to this friend—who was also in possession of the rest of faith—every minutia of my past experience, my conversion, after wanderings of heart, times of awakening, and again of relapse. God's special care and long-suffering amidst it all, seemed to come vividly to mind, and, at the remembrance, my soul melted before the Lord, when I suddenly awoke, while the room seemed filled with the glory of God, saying aloud, "In all this he has kept me to prove *his* UTMOST SALVATION; *his* FULLNESS *of* LOVE!" This made a deep impression on my mind, and was the means of intensifying my desires for holiness of heart.

My dear companion has of late also entered this rest of faith. May we be kept "steadfast, immovable, always abounding in the work of the Lord!"

January 11*th*. O, how fully is my soul proving, "There remaineth therefore a rest to the people of God," and "we which have believed do enter into rest!"

The land of Beulah is no longer in the distance, or a land enveloped in mist; nor is it where we catch but occasional glimpses of celestial light from a clouded sky; but it is a land from whose clear sky a bright steady light shines upon my pathway; an *increasing* light, as I journey onward, permeating my very being. Is not the pathway of the just as the shining light, that shineth more and more unto the perfect day? Then, why should Christians be talking ever of clouds and darkness? Is it not because they have wandered from the pathway of the just? O Thou, who hast called me out of darkness into thine own marvelous light, keep me; and, with thine own beams shining upon me, may I reflect ever the image of the heavenly!

May my experience never be like that of the moon in the allegory, who, in an eclipse, complained to the sun that his rays did not shine upon her as usual; but who, in searching out the cause, found that the earth was between them! O, how many such troubled souls at the present day! Go where we will, we find those whose complaint is, "I do not as in former days walk in the light of His countenance."* Know they not that the rays of the Sun of Righteousness are as warm and bright as ever, but the earth is between them and Christ?

January 14*th*. My soul has been much drawn out in prayer, of late, for closer communion with my Savior. Faith, hope, and love, all unite in saying, "I would see Jesus!"

"O, for a glimpse of him my soul adores!
As the chased hart, amid the desert waste,
Pants for the living stream: for Him who made her,
So pants the thirsty soul, amid the blank
Of sublunary joys."

O, the insufficiency of earthly things to satisfy the wants of the soul! Far beneath immortal minds are mortal pleasures. These longings for things more exalted—for higher, holier joys than earth can give—what are they? by whom given? when shall they be satisfied? IMMORTALITY, thou canst answer! In thee shall the highest aspirations be realized.

Knowing that these yearnings of soul were not given to mock, a Job, amid the fiery furnace, could hold still, while faith, looking through ages yet to come, exclaimed, "I know that my Redeemer liveth, and that he shall stand at the latter day upon the earth;" and, "Whom I shall see for myself, and mine eyes shall behold, and not another; though my reins be consumed within me." Nor are these yearnings for this fullness of joy, HERE, in vain. "For he SATISFIETH the longing soul, and filleth the hungry soul with goodness."

Feel that these breathings of soul after God, the living God, these desires to know more of Christ, have not been in vain. But O, I need a fresh anointing, a new baptism of the Holy Ghost! I must have it for the further establishment of my faith, and, above all, to fit me to labor more efficiently for the salvation of perishing souls. Have been permitted of late to see some precious ones gathered into the fold of Christ.

March 30*th.* The prayer for a new baptism has been answered. Last Thursday evening, while met with the people of God, with them awaiting the promise of the Father, I was blessed in a more powerful manner than ever before. Many others shared in this glorious baptism of the Holy Ghost. The meeting continued until near twelve. As Paul and Silas sang praises at midnight, so did we on that memorable night. If that were but a foretaste, what must the fountain be!

Truly, some of us felt that these frail bodies could bear no more, and live; but the language of our hearts was:

> "O, would He more of heaven bestow;
> And when the vessels break,
> Let our triumphant spirits go,
> To grasp the God we seek!"

April 23*d.* "For whatsoever is born of God overcometh the world: and this is the victory that overcometh the world, *even our faith.*" Satan hath desired to have me, that he might "sift me as wheat;" but One stronger hath said, "I have prayed for thee, that thy faith fail not." My all of strength was gone, but with the God-man I have prevailed. To him be glory!

For nearly a week past, have been proving the trial of my faith precious. Last evening, the contest seemed at its height, the adversary accusing me of having lost, or having never received, the blessing of "perfect love." Several days had been spent in fasting and prayer; but, seemingly, no advantage had been gained; and I resolved fully to commit my cause to the Conqueror, counting it "*all joy*" that I had fallen "into divers temptations; knowing that the trial of my faith would work patience," and that, if "patience had her perfect work," I, according to the promise, should be "perfect and entire, wanting nothing."

All around were locked in the embrace of sleep, the hour being late; and I took up my Bible, and opened to these words: "Wherefore I pray you to take some meat; for this is for your health: for there shall not a hair fall from the head of any of you." I immediately supplied the wants of the body, weak from continued fasting, and retired to rest; and was soon in a sweet sleep, and thought myself in the midst of a congregated world, all moved by some intense excitement. Some were in great consternation and fear, with anguish and remorse of mind depicted upon their countenances; others were calm and joyous. Wondering at the cause of all this, I looked in the direction in which the attention of all seemed riveted—the north-east—and beheld above the clouds the most beautiful light, beggaring all description—for earth has none such—which seemed to be encircling a city radiant with the glory within.

I watched it as it descended toward earth, at times lost in its own wondrous light, and thought of the description given by an inspired apostle: "And the city had no need of the sun, neither of the moon, to shine in it; for the glory of God did lighten it, and the Lamb is the light thereof. And the nations of them which are saved shall walk in the light of it: and the kings of the earth do bring their glory and honor into it;" and exclaimed, in an ecstasy of joy, "*It is the* NEW JERUSALEM, coming down from God out of heaven, prepared as a bride adorned for her husband!" while to me a voice from the city sweetly said, "*Him that* OVERCOMETH will I make a pillar in the temple of my God, and he shall go no more out;" and, "*He that overcometh shall inherit all things.*"

I quickly cast a glance upon my own garments, to see if I was ready to enter so pure a place, but could find no spots, while I exclaimed:

> "O love, thou bottomless abyss!
>   My sins are swallowed up in thee;
> Covered is my unrighteousness,
>   Nor spot of guilt remains on me:
> While JESUS' BLOOD, through earth and skies,
> Mercy, free, boundless mercy, cries;"

and with this awoke, but so filled with the presence of the Triune God as to be unable to sleep any more during the night. Heaven seemed so near; and, with an assurance unknown before, I can say, "The tabernacle of God is with men." To-day, my soul is inexpressibly happy.

> " By faith we already behold
>   That lovely Jerusalem here;

Her walls are of jasper and gold;
    As crystal, her buildings are clear.
Immovably founded in grace,
    She stands as she ever hath stood;
And brightly her Builder displays,
    And flames with the glory of God."

CHAPTER II.

JUNE 29TH. Have just been permitted to attend our district camp-meeting, at Quincy. Went with shrinkings of flesh, in view of crosses I felt would be mine to bear—crosses unusual, for at such gatherings I had hitherto been silent—yet with intense breathings of soul after God, and earnest desire and prayer for the welfare of our beloved Zion.

It was indeed a bethel to many souls. Some from our class, who had apparently opposed the spreading work of holiness in our midst, were brought low, and the Lord helped them. New witnesses were raised up of the efficacy of the blood of Christ to cleanse from the remains of the carnal mind. My triumphant soul exclaimed, as I looked upon the gracious work, "This is the Lord's doing, and it is marvelous in our eyes." To him be all the glory!

The Lord helped me to rise above my natural

timidity, and, as never before, to glory in the cross of Christ. I fully realized there is work for each to do. The fields already white to harvest, and the laborers so few! So many idlers; and yet work adapted to the strength of each! If we can not be a reaper, then a gleaner; if not a gleaner, there are child-errands to do. No one can say, "No man hath hired me." The command has been given, "Go ye also into the vineyard; and whatsoever is right, I will give you." ·That inactivity is not for the disciples of the lowly Nazarene, we are constantly admonished, from the time of a "I am slow of speech," contending with "I AM hath sent thee," to "Behold, I send you forth as sheep among wolves;" "As the Father hath sent me, even so send I you." But with these commands we hear ever the voice of the Master, "Lo, I am with you alway."

"The glorious privilege, TO DO,
Is man's most noble dower."

One day, at this long-to-be-remembered meeting, I had been absent from our tent most of the day, doing what little I could for the cause of Christ, leaving the care of our little Ella, not yet three years of age, to others, and so intent was my soul in its work that for the time she was forgotten; when suddenly the tempter, ever ready, insinuated that in my anxiety for others I was neglecting my own work; that my first care should be for my own. I immediately hastened to the tent, and, as she met me at its door, inquired of her, in a playful manner, "Who is your keeper?" Her ready answer, in childish accents, of, "*The Lord is my keeper!*" assured my heart that I was to

> "Fix on His work my steadfast eye,
> So should my work be done."

O, as I journey onward in the path of obedience, I see more and more of the simple way of faith. How ready is our great Teacher to teach us, when we are but willing to lay aside our own wisdom and be taught!

June 1, 1862. A long time has passed since any record has here been made of the dealings of an ever-kind Heavenly Father with my soul. But upon memory's tablet are its scenes, both of trial and gladness, engraved.

O, it is wise to talk with our past hours, and ask them what report they have borne to heaven, what record have they made in eternity? With confidence I look up, knowing that my treasures are accumulating in the better land. Earthly honors, pleasures, and emulations have lost their power to woo this heart. These are 'mid the darkness of the past.

> "There is my house and portion fair;
> My treasure and my heart are there,
> And my abiding home."

Have, during these two years, been brought very near death's door. But, while "to live is Christ," to die "is gain." The sting of death, which is sin—death has no sting beside—through my Conquering King, was all removed; while, with faith's clear vision, I looked beyond the tide. O, there were beauties just over the river! There, living waters were flowing, palms of glory waving, raiment white decking the saints! There my soul would no more have known the exile's thirst. But my crown! TOO FEW WERE ITS SRARS! and again I have been permitted, with renewed courage, to take my cross.

> "Once again beside the cross,
> All my gain I count but loss;
> Earthly pleasures fade away,
> Clouds they are that hide my day.
> Hence, vain shadows; let me see
> Jesus crucified for me."

But death has entered our family circle, bearing away one ripe for the better land. Mother Page is no more. For over a year, she seemed to mortal eye standing upon the verge of Jordan, brushing with her feet its heavy dews. But, amid great suffering, she could say:

> "My cheerful soul now, all the day,
> Sits waiting here, and sings;
> Looks through the ruin of her clay,
> And practices her wings.
> Faith almost changes into sight,
> While from afar she spies
> Her fair inheritance in light,
> Above created skies."

For many years, she went in and out before us, exemplifying by precept and example the power of our holy Christianity; and, when brought low by the hand of disease, with confidence could say: "I know whom I have believed;" "I know that my Redeemer liveth." In her own words, the veil seemed oft parted while in blissful anticipation she looked upon the joys of the redeemed. She rests from her labors, and her works do follow her. We'll meet thee, mother, where sorrow and suffering are unknown.

July 16*th*. Have felt, of late, very much interested in the spiritual welfare of the members of my Bible-class. A short time since, the duty of appointing a weekly meeting for their benefit was presented to my mind.

My heart has been much drawn out in prayer

since its appointment, that, if this were of the Lord, our first meeting might be SPECIALLY favored with the Divine presence. Eight young ladies were present, all but one professors, and her we were permitted to carry to the Father as an earnest seeker of the "pearl of great price." All took a part in the exercises; though it was with trembling, I called upon some to pray, as I had never heard their voices in our social meetings. Some with tears spoke of their unfaithfulness and desire for a deeper work of grace. May the good Shepherd bless these lambs of his fold, and lead them nearer to himself! O, for grace and wisdom from above to enable me to say to these, "Follow me even as I follow Christ!" I greatly desire that by experience they may know of the blessedness of forsaking *all* for Christ. Read to them to-day, from Mrs. Palmer's "Entire Devotion," of the happy life and triumphant death of one who had thus in early life counted the cost of coming out from the world and being separate. O, that there was more holy living among those who have been long in the way! With how much greater success could we then point the young convert to the "fountain opened in the house of David and to the inhabitants of Jerusalem, for sin and uncleanness." But God be praised that there *are* many living members in his Church—

"polished stones," who reflect the image of Christ. May the number be greatly increased!

August 1st. Have been struggling, for some time past, with the powers of darkness. How true that we "wrestle not against flesh and blood," but "against principalities, against powers, against the rulers of the darkness of this world, against spiritual wickedness in high places." But the Word of the Lord is my strong tower: "A bruised reed shall he not break and smoking flax shall he not quench, till he send forth judgment unto victory." Have not, for some time past, felt as clear a sense of constant abiding in Christ as I believe to be my privilege. Am humbled in the dust in view of my own nothingness.

> "I loathe myself when God I see,
> And into nothing fall;
> Content if thou exalted be,
> And Christ be all in all."

O, I must be more like Christ! The baptism of the Holy Spirit—for this my soul looks up! I thirst! Spring up, O well, I ever cry, spring up within this soul! O, wash me, and I shall be "whiter than snow!" Nothing less than thine own nature can satisfy. Give me thyself! Had I all things else, without THEE I were a wretch undone. "Without *faith*, it is impossible to please

God." "Abraham BELIEVED God, and it was counted unto him for righteousness." "The just shall live BY FAITH." Passages like these are much on my mind. Feel a consciousness of being led by the Spirit of God: "For as many as are led by the Spirit of God, they are the sons of God." Yes, I *am* thy child! *Thou*—O joy!—art my Father!

> "In hope believing against hope,
> Jesus, my Lord, my God, I claim."

August 30*th*. Have been permitted, during this month, to meet God's people in the tented grove, in Albion District. O, consecrated ground! Delightful place where God meets his chosen Israel! Have been consciously brought into closer union and communion with Him whom my soul loveth.

> "O, in the secret of His presence dwelleth
> FULLNESS OF JOY, forever and forever!"

Yet shades of sorrow seem falling about my pathway. "Sorrowful, yet always rejoicing!" Storms of wrath are shaking our nation. Sacrifices of blood are being lain upon our altars. To human sight the future is enshrouded in darkness and mystery. Can I say, welcome alike the crown or cross? This morning took up, for comfort, the ever-blessed Word. My eye rested upon, "Ye shall drink indeed of my cup, and be baptized with the baptism that I am baptized with." What means it? Is it to be *sorrow*, that

> "Shall build the shining ladder up,
> Whose golden rounds are our calamities,
> Whereon our firm feet planting, NEARER GOD
> The spirit climbs, and hath its eyes unsealed?"

January 27th, 1863. Strange have been the scenes and trials through which I have passed during the last few months. On the sixteenth of December, ult., feeling that God called for the sacrifice, my companion enlisted in the service of his country. Long have we felt that true freedom was not alone to break

> "Fetters for our own dear sake,
> And, with leathern hearts, forget
> That we owe mankind a debt."

And now, when such important results—the freedom of our land from traitors, the breaking of the tyrant's chain, and the proclaiming of liberty to the captive—were at stake, I could not selfishly say, "*Stay!*" Oft in the past, when gathered in our happy family group, from our consecrated altar has ascended the fervent prayer, "*Let the* OPPRESSED *go free.*" And now I dare not refuse my offering to the onward march of liberty, even though that march be through seas of blood.

> "God moves in a mysterious way,
> His wonders to perform."

O Thou, who makest even the wrath of man to praise thee, and who hath promised that not a sparrow shall fall to the ground without our Father, to thee I look! O, thou shadow of a great rock in a weary land, be thou my hiding-place; and, although

> " Pain's furnace-heat within me quivers,
> God's breath upon the flames doth blow,
> And all my heart in anguish shivers,
> And trembles at the fiery glow,"—

yet O, help me calmly to whisper, "God's will be done!"

> "And in his hottest fire HOLD STILL!"

Thank God! I have left me the calm, safe, and sure retreat beneath the mercy-seat. Never before did I so realize the power of prayer to calm the troubled heart. Blessed assurance, that we have not an High-priest who can not be "touched with the feeling of our infirmities."

February 5*th*. We have to-day taken the parting hand, not knowing when we shall meet again. Perhaps never on earth! How can I bear the thought? O, thou sympathizing Savior, leave me not! Remember I am dust.

February 22*d*. My mind seems constantly occupied with one thought, "that the regiment in which my companion is, to-day moves toward the scene of strife." Is it true we are to be so far separated, and perhaps never meet again until the morning of the resurrection? But hush, O my soul! "Clouds and darkness are round about him;" yet knew I that there is a heaven-side to the dark cloud o'ershadowing our beloved country. From that side, hidden to mortal vision, comes the soothing whisper, "Righteousness and judgment are the habitation of His throne."

We SHALL meet again; if not on earth, at the marriage-supper of the Lamb, and, with the blood-washed millions, join in the new song.

March 22*d.* The holy Sabbath, sweet emblem of eternal rest. Have been permitted to-day to sit under the droppings of the sanctuary, and felt strengthened to walk the narrow way—the way I know I love. From CHOICE, I tread its paths. No lion treads it; no ravenous beast goes up thereon; and, all praise to Him who trod it before me, the "vulture's eye" hath not seen it, but on it the "ransomed of the Lord shall return, and come to Zion with songs and everlasting joy upon their heads: they shall obtain joy and gladness, and SORROW AND SIGHING SHALL FLEE AWAY."

Storms of wrath are still shaking earth and sea. There are cries of "Lo, here!" and "Lo, there!" but onward I'll haste. There is light ahead. It gleams from the city of which "glorious things are spoken;" "Beautiful for situation, the joy of the whole earth."

June 29th. Have again been permitted to meet God's people on the old camp-ground at Quincy. Had here no joyous, ecstatic emotions, but all through the meeting seemed before me in legible characters, " *The just shall live by* FAITH !" Upon this I rested SATISFIED. It seemed at the time that if all else of the Word of God were forever blotted out, with this I could still journey onward, even though my onward march be *alone*, through storm after storm. This morning I awoke, very happy in God. In my night visions, I thought myself with a dear Christian friend in a lonely wood, unweariedly journeying onward, when unexpectedly we came upon a deep thicket of thorns. Suddenly my friend disappeared, and I next saw her upon the other side beyond the hedge, in a most lovely place, where were shady trees, green pastures, rivers of clear water, singing birds, and every thing attractive. With uplifted hands and streaming eyes, she was praising God for delivering grace, while I was exerting every power to extricate myself from the thorns which, turn which way I would, were lacerating my flesh and tearing and blackening my dress of clear white. After many endeavors, I succeeded in extricating myself from the hedge and reaching my friend. Upon examining my garments I found them perfectly whole and of a purer white than when I entered the thorns. At this we were filled with wonder, and together we joined in songs of praise to our Deliverer. Father, grant that thus it may be; that from amid the fiery trials of earth I may come forth without even the mark or smell of fire upon my garments!

"To Him mine eye of faith I turn,
And through the fire pursue my way;
The fire forgets its power to burn,
The lambent flames around me play;
I own His power, accept the sign,
And shout to prove the Savior mine."

This has been a precious day to my soul; am being brought into closer union with Christ. The sweet consciousness which I feel of an abiding in Christ, is inexpressible. The half was never told. Would that I could tell the story of redeeming grace and dying love! Glorious thought, that by and by this tongue will be unloosed!

"Then in a nobler, sweeter song, .
I'll sing Thy power to save."

CHAPTER III.

APRIL 27, 1864. Have suffered much in mind of late, in reference to my companion. Scarcely a week passes but that the news of some of our friends fallen, reaches us. The habiliments of woe are all around us. The orphans' tears, the widows' weeds and sighs, the mourning for fallen brothers, every-where remind us that war and bloodshed are in our land; yet the strife ceaseth not. The great armies are soon to move. Hearts, with anguish, are yet to be rent in twain. A few nights since, I dreamed of attending my dear T.'s funeral. My sorrow seemed so great as to unable me to support myself, and I was carried into the church by others. In passing through the aisle (the congregation were all seated before I entered the house), among the group of mourners I discovered Mother P. She had a countenance unearthly in all respects. Such perfect calmness and holy joy I never saw upon the face of mortal. Her dress was of pure white. I gazed upon her, and wondered how she could be so unmoved—and my anguish so great!

I heard nothing of the sermon; but at its close a group of white negroes, also clad in snow-white garments, more lovely than earth can boast—though I knew them to be of the despised race—came, and, standing before me, commenced singing. The words (there were a number of verses) I heard distinctly. It seemed to be not the composition of earth, excepting the chorus, which was:

"*There is* SWEET REST, SISTER, FOR THEE IN HEAVEN."

The music I will not attempt to describe. Earth has no words in which to speak of it. As they sang verse after verse, I commenced shouting—first in a whisper; then, rising higher and higher—"GLORY TO GOD!" until I awoke with the thought, "I am shouting at my husband's funeral."

May 11*th*. All around is quietness. The hour is late, yet I can not sleep. The armies have met. Thousands have fallen. No letter yet! This morning awoke, repeating:

"My lifted eye, without a tear,
 The gath'ring storm shall see;

> My steadfast heart shall know no fear;
> That heart will rest on Thee."

Never before was I so lifted above earth. This afternoon, Rev. H. Law called. Had a season of prayer. Brother Law prayed much for dear husband. Said, in his prayer, "Lord, we give him to his country." I could not respond or pray, only continue silently to repeat:

> "My lifted eye, without a tear."

So completely, this day, have I been lifted above the world and its sorrows, that it has seemed that if at any moment the news should come, "Truman is fallen," it would not have moved me from my perfect calmness and rest of soul. This evening, tried to pray, as usual, for his safety and return to the embrace of his family, but could not. My only prayer was, that if he were suffering in the land of the enemy, the Lord would raise up some one to care for him. Long the struggle continued, until it was said, "*Thy* PRAYER *is* HEARD."

July 10*th*. Again I take my pen. But O, where shall I begin, or with what words shall I record the scenes through which I have passed of late?

Eighteen months since, and ours was a happy, unbroken family circle. Can it be that now I am left to write, "My CHILDREN FATHERLESS, and I A WIDOW?" But I no longer pray, "Let this cup pass from me!" I drink it, and know it is well; for my Father's hand, though unseen, prepared it.

For eighteen months have we watched anxiously, amid our country's night, for the breaking of the morning when, the war ended, husband and father would be again safe at home. That will never come! What do I write? Ah, yes: it HAS come! He is *safe* AT HOME; and through my tears I still look forward to a brighter, more glorious morning than ever dawned upon this sorrow-stricken earth, that shall give me back the not lost, but gone before.

> "O, heaven is where no secret dread
> May haunt love's meeting hour;
> Where from the past no gloom is shed
> O'er the heart's chosen bower;
> Where every severed wreath is bound,
> And none have heard the knell
> That smites the soul in that wild sound:
> FAREWELL, BELOV'D, FAREWELL."

On the twenty-third of May, in reference to that dear one, came these few words, "MORTALLY WOUNDED ON THE ELEVENTH." Ah! who that hath not FELT it, knoweth the anguish hidden in those two words? Then, a few days after, written by a friend and companion at his side:

"I was the first to reach your husband after he fell. I found him suffering intensely; spoke of moving him off the field. He replied, '*No; let me die on the field of battle;*' then looked up, and, with joy and animation unspeakable beaming in his countenance, added: '*O Sergeant, you don't know how happy I am! Tell Emily not to mourn for Truman;* for it is all right. I die happy.'"

This was while making a rapid raid on the enemy's ground, and he, with others, had to be left; left dying—never to be heard from more, as the wound was known to be mortal. Friends, brothers in Christ and companions in arms, gathered around and hastily took the parting hand, speaking with regret of leaving him thus. He replied, "*It is no matter; we shall soon meet in heaven.*"

The LITTLE LEFT to do for the dead has been done. In a changed world, we made preparations for the funeral services; and gathered in our village church, where we had long worshiped together, and at whose altar he gave his heart to God. And as our loved pastor—Rev. H. Law—with tearful eye and choked utterance, read for the text, "There the wicked cease from troubling and the weary are at rest;" and the choir sang, "Let me die on the field of battle," from the "Guide to Holiness," which he had loved at home and in the army, and " There's a light in the window for thee, sister;" we felt that there were angels hovering round us,

"Unperceived amid the throng;"

and though, perhaps, some saw but the sad funeral tapers, WE caught glimpses of heaven's distant lamps.

"Over the river they beckoned to me,
 Loved ones who had crossed to the further side;
The gleam of their snowy robes I could see,
 But their voices were lost in the dashing tide."

Ah, Truman! THOU art 'mid the shining throng; I amid the sorrowing! Thy life-borne cross hath carried thee beyond the reach of change and suffering! Beyond the stormy battle-field, thou art triumphing now! The "star-spangled banner" thou didst love; but with thee, ever placed just ABOVE the "glorious stars and stripes," was the standard of the cross, with the Christian's motto, "VICTORY THROUGH THE BLOOD OF THE LAMB!" THAT victory thou hast gained. O, what a change! From the battle-field, after days of weary marching, into the presence of God, to behold his glory! Thy far-off grave, in lands unknown, I may never visit, there to weep; but that glorious day, of which thy pen, in thy last missive to the absent, spake, "when Christ shall come to make up his jewels," will soon come; then thy grave will be found by him who watches all thy dust until he shall bid it rise and put on immortality! Until then I wait; wait, watching for the morning when the dead shall wake.

August 9th. Another month of sadness. The storms of earth are passing, wafting my little bark nearer and nearer the haven of eternal rest.

Since writing last, have received intelligence, by open letter from Richmond, that my husband was taken prisoner, carried to R., lived seven days, and then passed away, with the dying message on his lips, "TELL MY FAMILY TO MEET ME IN HEAVEN.;" and thitherward I'm journeying.

> "Thou knowest, in the spirit of prayer,
> We long thy appearing to see;
> Resigned to the burden we bear,
> But longing to triumph with thee."

Our national affairs are growing darker and darker. The protracted dry weather in many parts seems threatening our land with famine. But "OUR FATHER'S AT THE HELM." Faith catches glimpses of light in the distance. "The Lord reigneth; let the earth rejoice." "He that dwelleth in the secret place of the Most High shall abide under the shadow of the Almighty." "God is our refuge and strength, a very present help in trouble. Therefore will not we fear, though the earth be removed, and though the mountains be carried into the midst of the sea; though the waters thereof roar and be troubled, though the mountains shake with the swelling thereof."

Have been blessed with many comforts of late—fellowship with kindred minds, and messages of Christian sympathy from friends highly esteemed. Among these was a deeply interesting letter from Rev. J. Boynton, of Manistee District. He had just read the notice of my dear husband's death, and hastened to comfort me; and well did he perform his mission. He speaks of him as not being SLAIN, but as only having DEPARTED this life to be with Christ, which is far better; says, when I think of him I need not think of his coffin, his winding-sheet, or his grave, but as a glorified spirit; and that I hope very soon to meet that loved one, where

"The dirge-like sound of parting words
Shall smite the soul no more."

Thank Heaven, this consolation IS mine! He writes: "I was led to rejoice as the notice of the death of brother Page brought you to my mind, as I thought, 'She enjoys full salvation through the blood of the Lamb.'" O, how that sentence caused deep heart-searching before God! And long after the silence of night had hushed all around into quietness, the searching went on.

When we last met, I could say with confidence, as he now writes, "*My witness is clear; the blood of Christ cleanseth me;*" but, amid the sorrows of the past two years, I should fear to say, "In all this I have offended not." Fear mine has been too much the sorrow of the world, which "worketh death." Yet, God is my witness, I have desired his glory above all earthly good. But O, the weakness of the flesh! God help me, now and forever, to renounce all strength but strength Divine! O, I gain nothing by this looking at self! Compassionate Redeemer, I lift mine eye to thee! Thou liftest the mourner from the dust. O, satisfy the longings of this tempest-tossed soul, and make me more like thyself! I want the witness that all I do, all I say, and all I FEEL, meets the Divine approval. I ask no higher state than this. 'T is enough.

> "Lord, shall the breathings of my heart
> Aspire in vain to thee?"

No! no! Thou wilt perform in me the promise of thy Son.

October 2d. The blessings of the sanctuary have to-day been most precious to my soul. "One thing have I desired of the Lord, that will I seek after; that I may dwell in the house of the Lord all the days of my life, to behold the beauty of the Lord, and to inquire in his temple. For in the *time of* TROUBLE *he shall* HIDE *me in his* PAVILION: in the secret of his tabernacle shall he hide me: he shall set me up upon a rock."

Nearly five months since, the body of my husband was laid by the hand of the enemy beneath a Southern soil. But it is a Christian's grave; and, borne on the breeze wafted from that Southern clime, comes a gentle whisper, "Not here, but risen; tell my family to meet me in heaven."

A friend, who is alike passing through the furnace, a few days since handed me the following lines, to us so expressive:

"O, mourning one, watching 'mid our country's night,
For footsteps which come not; O, look to the light!
On distant and bloody fields, piled with the slain,
They sleep, who were folded within thy heart's fane.
Above their damp pillow thou never may'st weep,
No tear-drop shall waken the hero's last sleep,
Yet mourn not. The angels, from climes of the blest,
With pitying footfall, are guarding their rest:
And, though the storm howleth, and wint'ry winds rave
Through snowy veil, there is light on the grave;

> For soft as the angels tread on the dark sod,
> There lingers a radiance which brightens the clod.
> Deep sorrow has shrouded the sun's joyous light;
> No pitying Luna steps into thy night;
> Yet on the dark curtain of thy troubled skies
> Stands a little star-promise, 'THY HUSBAND SHALL RISE!'"

Upon that star the eye of faith is fixed. It shines with a steady lustrous light. With this above it, the grave has lost its gloom. "O death! where is thy sting? O grave! where is thy victory?"

My heart loses none of its sadness, yet I believingly read, "Blessed are they that mourn;" "For our light affliction which is but for a moment, worketh for us a far more exceeding and eternal weight of glory!" I am kept from all my fears, and my lonely home is cheered by the presence of the Unseen, and oft becomes a bethel to my soul. O, the victories of the Cross of Christ!

> "A sovereign balm for every wound;
> A cordial for our fears."

January 20, 1865. Time is hastening on. Our life is even "a vapor, that appeareth for a little time, and then vanisheth away."

> "No matter which my thoughts employ,
> A moment's misery or joy;
> But O, when both shall end,
> Where shall I find my destined place?
> Shall I my everlasting days
> With fiends or angels spend?"

J. S., a prisoner from Richmond and Andersonville, a former friend of my companion, and a resident of our place, has returned, bringing the further particulars of the death of my husband.

O, how clearly do I see in him the answer of the prayer of that ever-to-be-remembered day, May 11, 1864—a friend raised up in the land of a cruel enemy, in direct answer to prayer, to care for the wants of a dying Christian soldier! God be praised! Tears of gratitude, of thanksgiving and praise to our Father in heaven, whose SPECIAL PROVIDENCE is over his own, course down my cheeks. After the regiment left, my companion revived; the next day, was taken prisoner, and carried to Richmond. J. S., being there a prisoner, was detailed for service in the hospital of our men, and was called upon to assist in carrying him from the ambulance, in which he was brought to Richmond, to his bed. In going up the second flight of stairs my husband recognized him, reached out to him his hand, calling him by name. From that moment, J. S. stood by him as a brother, doing all in his power to alleviate his sufferings during the six days he tarried upon earth. Of him, he says: " He never once, amid his pain and suffering, spoke of it, but was almost continually, during waking moments, giving vent to the joy within in praises to God ; and, when dying, took the weeping soldiers around him—sufferers together in the land of the enemy—separately by the hand, and mingled with thanks for their kindness to him exhortations to meet him in heaven; and when the tongue became palsied and silent in death, he raised himself on his couch, and, with both hands pointed upward, sank back, and SLEPT IN JESUS! And though no earthly companion, father, mother, brother or sister was there to smooth that dying pillow, again was proved, as it has been on so many a battle-field, in hospitals and loathsome prisons, that

> 'Jesus can make a dying bed
> Feel soft as downy pillows are,
> While on his breast we lean our head,
> And breathe our life out sweetly there.'"

Death was once again despoiled of its sting and the grave of its victory; and, though long accustomed to look upon the dreariness of the rebel prison and hospital as without equal, I can only now think of it as one of the bright spots of earth, where the spirit of my dear one passed up to the realms of day. O no: to *him* there was no gloom there.

> "Glory had chased away the gloom,
> For Christ had conquered there."

Long I watched for the coming of his footsteps here. I wait and watch no longer. Two, of such of whom the Savior said, "Suffer" them, "and forbid them not, to come unto me," have ceased to ask, "WHEN WILL PAPA COME?" but up yonder, in our Father's mansion, where there is plenty of light, he waits and watches for us; and, with my eye steadily fixed upon the eternal Word, "The just shall live by faith," I press forward. Mine eyes shall yet see "Jerusalem a quiet habitation, a tabernacle that shall not be taken down; not one of the stakes thereof shall ever be removed, neither shall any of the cords thereof be broken." J. S. is earnestly seeking the salvation of his soul. Is a young man of much promise. Dates his convictions to that happy death-bed scene in a Richmond hospital. Ah, dear T.! brighter stars than ever decked the brow of an earthly conqueror are thine.

April 10*th*. Memorable evening! O, what joy is in our land.! While I write, cannons are being fired; in every direction bells are mingling in wild harmony with the grandeur of the scene. "THE WAR ENDED!" is the cry. Lee has surrendered. Notes of victory every-where are heard; and why seek I the seclusion of my room? O, why can not I, too, mingle with the joyous throng? HIS battle's fought; the victory he hath won. Looketh not THAT ONE down from glory upon this scene? And though he cometh not with the greeting so long looked for; though, while hearts to-night beat high with the joy within, mine in sadness lingereth at a far-off grave, where lieth but dust,—shall I not join in the anthem upon the air, "REJOICE! HE HATH DONE ALL THINGS WELL?" O Father! to thee I lift my tearful eye and heart of anguish. Are not the tears of the widows and orphans of our land shed to-night, bottled up? Cry they not unto thee? "And shall not God avenge his own elect which cry day and night unto him, though he bear long with them?" I hear the answer: "Shall not the Judge of all the earth do right?" Thy purposes are already ripening. O, how they have been unfolding to our astonished nation during these years of bloodshed and sufferings! In my sorrows I see the hand of God. Complete the purposes of thy will.

September 3d. A long time has passed, and nothing has been written of the precious dealings of God with me. Time has been so fully occupied as to leave but little opportunity for pursuits most loved and prized; but is not this discipline of mind needed? I joyfully yield what most I prize, to Him,

> "Who never has a good withheld,
> Or will withhold from me."

My mind is being kept in uninterrupted peace. How rich the legacy, "Peace I leave with you; my peace I give unto you; not as the world giveth give I unto you!" "Let not your heart be troubled, neither let it be afraid." Here I *rest*. I know not the future; can not see to take one step; but with confidence I look up, and say, "Father, I am blind; lead me!"

Was permitted, last month, to rest for a few days from my arduous school duties and attend the Quincy Camp-meeting. Went, feeling that it would be but to suffer; so much to bring remembrances of the past, when *one* sang with us the songs of Zion in that consecrated grove, whose place on earth is now forever vacant, who now sings the song of the redeemed with the multitude around the Throne. But I would here record to the glory of God's grace, that that grace wonderfully triumphed. Earth no longer fettering the soul, faith in the Unseen brought us near "unto Mount Sion, and unto the city of the living God, the heavenly Jerusalem, and to an innumerable company of angels, to the general assembly and Church of the first-born, which are written in heaven, and to God the Judge of all, and to the spirits of just men made perfect; and to Jesus, the mediator of the new covenant; and to the blood of sprinkling;" and looking away from the far-off graves of buried friends, we beheld in this Mediator the connecting ladder betwixt earth and heaven:

> "Ah! methinks there is a union,
>   There are ties which heavenward draw;
> Faith reveals, in clearest vision,
>   Just the ladder Jacob saw;"

and on its golden rounds we climb, until

> "By faith we join our hands
>   With those that went before;
> And greet the blood besprinkled bands
>   On the eternal shore."

Was this all imagination, but an idle chimera of the brain, that made our communion with the heavenly throng so precious in that leafy temple?

And God be praised that here also, in walking forward in the path of obedience, my soul found the perfect rest it so much desired! Glory to God above! The waters, so long overwhelming my soul, are ceasing. The swift-returning dove is bringing home signs of peace. He hath "removed me out of a strait into a broad place, where there is no straitness." The Spirit made so clear to me what was lacking on my part: that, "with the heart man believeth unto righteousness; and with the mouth confession is made unto salvation." For some time past, my witness not being clear, I have been careful not to speak definitely of the work accomplished in the soul; but, in an unlooked-for manner, was brought out of my lurking-place.

I stood, on the second day of the meeting, amid a group who were earnestly discussing the subject of full salvation. I had been a silent listener, when, unexpectedly, a brother turned to me with the interrogation, "Sister Page, do you enjoy the blessing of perfect love?"

For a moment I was silent; but felt that to say no would greatly dishonor my Savior; and, casting myself anew upon the atoning blood, tremblingly replied, "I would not dare say I do not; I am daring to reckon myself 'dead indeed unto sin, but alive unto God, through Jesus Christ our Lord.'"

From that moment, no doubts were mine. Power, beyond that hitherto possessed, was given to labor in the vineyord, to help those desiring to find the way of holiness; so that I seemed continually a wonder to myself.

O, the blessedness of this "highway!" I love of late to call it the path of obedience—a constant walking, simply in "the light." This to me so fully expresses it. The light may be feeble at first; but a moving forward brings the increase.

"Walk in the light; and thou shalt own
Thy darkness passed away,

> Because that light hath on thee shone,
> In which is perfect day."

"If we walk in the light as he is in the light, we have fellowship one with another; and the blood of Jesus Christ his Son cleanseth us from all sin;" not hath cleansed, or will cleanse, but cleanseth.

THE TRIAL AND VICTORY.

THE last night of this meeting had come; and, from the victories already achieved in the name of our Conquering King, glorious results were expected. It being stormy, we gathered in a large tent prepared for the occasion; but Eternal Wisdom, who seeth not as man seeth, chose that by the trial of our faith glory should come unto his name. The first of the evening was spent in listening to an earnest sermon from one who during the meeting had entered the rest of faith; but a darkness that could be felt seemed to settle upon the speaker and congregation.

At its close, a prayer-meeting was commenced; but spiritual power was lacking, and many of us felt that help must speedily come from God, or the last night of our meeting would be a failure, when we had asked for and expected triumph through Israel's Redeemer.

Our soul was unusually burdened; and so great were the temptations of the adversary that, had we dared, we should have left the tent.

Opportunity was given for speaking; but the darkness seemed but to increase.

We arose simply to frustrate the designs of the tempter in our case, and, while every word seemed withstood by the powers of darkness, repeated in strong language our consecration vows, saying, notwithstanding his insinuations, "From this moment, we live or die to serve our God alone;" and sat down with our burden but increased, until it seemed the frail body could endure no more.

Entering into a silent struggle of prayer for victory to come to our tent, we were lost to all around, until our own voice, crying aloud for victory, was heard above the silence that had fallen upon us. Moved as never before, and greatly to our humiliation, we exhorted those around us who had the meeting in charge to hold on to the promises of God by faith, and victory would be ours. Here the adversary endeavored to close our mouth by the interrogation, "What will your friends think of you?" I felt they would be greatly tried, and in agony of soul cried out, "Let me sink into the dust, but let God be glorified!" and, but for the support of friends, would have fallen to the ground. At that moment the Lord took the work into his own hands, and glorious were the victories of that night.

Person after person, by name, was presented to our mind; and, calling aloud upon God for his blessing. upon them, without exception they came and bowed with us, and travailed in soul until the baptism of the Holy Ghost fell upon them.

During this, our mind was intently fixed upon those whom God had so wonderfully laid upon our soul, and upon looking up for the first, what was our astonishment and humiliation to find the congregation standing, gathered around, and looking, some with wonder, upon this unusual demonstration; and among the number a young lady in whose salvation we had become prayerfully and intensely interested. As we saw her looking upon this, to her, strange scene, the adversary tauntingly suggested, "This will drive her conviction all away; you can have no more influence over her to lead her to the cross of Christ." But what was our joy as, a few moments after, she, unsolicited, threw herself upon her knees at our side, begging us to pray for her; and then, with strong cries and tears, began pleading for salvation, and thus continued until the garment of mourning was exchanged for that of rejoicing!

Cries for God's mercy now arose from every part of the tent, strong ones in faith and prayer going back and forth amid the congregation, pointing the sinner to the "Lamb of God which taketh away the sin of the world," and the hungry and thirsty soul to the "open fountain."

Never before were we so completely humbled, and never before did we so fully recognize the power of God working in the weak "to confound the things which are mighty, that no flesh should glory in his presence," but in Christ, "who of God is made unto us wisdom and righteousness and sanctification and redemption."

CHAPTER IV.

SEPTEMBER 18TH. Under the last date, the third, I wrote, surrounded with precious society and influences, at the home of our beloved presiding elder, Rev. R. C. Crawford, at Coldwater. The week spent with my dear friends, sisters Crawford and Trauger, and others at that place, will forever be remembered as one of the green spots in life's journey. How sweet the communion of kindred minds! True it is, "Their fellowship is like to that above." Had heaven no other attraction, this were sufficient inducement for a pressing forward. O, how precious these way-side resting-places, these soul-communings, to the lone, burdened heart! There is power in words of kindness; "apples of gold" are they, "in pictures of silver." They make earth more a heaven. Father, help me to scatter these wherever I go: freely as I have received, freely give!

Have seen, of late, great meaning in the words of Inspiration: "Behold I have refined thee, but not with silver; I have chosen thee in the furnace of affliction;" and have felt it, as one has said, an honor such as the worldly-minded comprehendeth not to be thus chosen; to have the dearest, best one of the household taken to dwell with Himself. And I have thought, in reference to that one watching for our coming on the other shore, that perhaps he is looking on with interest and joy to the erection of our mansion there; that the overcoming of every trial and temptation may add a new polished stone to that house made without hands, and be another cause for songs of triumph from that one saved forever from the storms of earth.

The Detroit Conference held its annual session last week. My father, Rev. J. Dobbins, has again placed himself on the effective list (having been, on account of ill health, superannuated the past four years), and has received an appointment to Waterloo and Franciscoville. They will move soon; and, if the Lord will, I shall soon follow them to their field of labor. I go from choice—from a desire to be useful. My pleasant home and surroundings have strong attractions; but they are nothing compared with those of our Father's house, where there are "many mansions." There I'll lay up my treasures.

> "'T is hid from view; but we may guess
> How beautiful that realm may be
> For gleamings of its loveliness
> In visions granted oft we see."

Time is short: what is done must be done quickly. And what matters it whether our head be pillowed upon down or stone? whether we travel over rough and thorny ways, or beside still waters, in green pastures? Christ, our Anointed, "the same yesterday, to-day, and forever," hath said, "I will never leave thee nor forsake thee." Zion is our secure resting-place. All her foes shall be confounded; and, though millions of worlds should combine against her, "My people," saith He that sitteth between the cherubim, "shall dwell in a peaceable habitation, and in sure dwellings, and in quiet resting-places." And satisfied, with no fear of want, drinking of the pure "river of water of life, clear as crystal," and eating of the "tree of life," the leaves of which are for the "healing of the nations," where He appoints we go, glorying in nothing save the cross of Christ. And when our work is done, with the now Church militant and Church triumphant, which are one, we'll lay our trophies at his feet. Until then,

> "In the desert let me labor,
> On the mountain let me tell
> How he died, the blessed Savior,
> To redeem a world from hell."

MRS. C. E. M'ALLISTER.*

HAVE just learned of the death of a dear friend, Mrs. C. E. M'Allister, one who, for over twelve years, has been a sharer in the joys and sorrows of the itinerant life; of whom it might well be said:

> "None knew thee but to love;
> None named thee but to praise."

But the tie of earth is severed, or, rather, the mysterious chain uniting her spirit to kindred ones upon earth is *not* severed, only lengthened, until its links have reached God's throne.

But a few days before the crown that shines immortal was placed upon her brow, to her it was said of an only child, a son of eleven:

> "The Lord has need of this floweret gay! . . .
> And the mother gave in tears and pain,
> The flower she much did love:
> She knew she would find it SOON again
> In the fields of light above."

*Wife of Rev. J. E. M'Allister, Michigan Conference.

But a few hours before his death, when all thought him gone, and his mother, hiding her face in his pillow, sobbingly exclaimed, "Joey is gone; his sufferings are ended!" he suddenly looked up, and said, "Do n't cry, mamma; I am better now!" and soon after, as his happy spirit passed away to his home where bright angels are now folding him close beneath their glittering wings, with a smile upon his face, "Good-bye, papa! good-bye, mamma! I am going home."

The Healer was near, pouring balm upon the mother's heart, and very calmly she bowed to the will of Him who doeth all things well, as the reaper death carried from her embrace her darling boy, and placed him, the "planted in the house of the Lord," safely "in the courts of our God above," and then hastened on another mission to earth, and to the stricken father said, "I have come for the mother of thy boy!"

> "There is weeping on earth for the lost!
> There is bowing in grief to the ground!
> But rejoicing and praise 'mid the sanctified host,
> For a spirit in paradise found! . . ,
> And a new harp is strung, and a new song is given
> To the breezes that float o'er the gardens of heaven!"

As she neared the valley of the "shadow of death," as one moistened her lips with water, she replied, "How good; but not as good as the river, 'the streams whereof make glad the city of our

God!'" then pointing with her hand, "There! Joey has come! Joey has come for me!" A sister standing by, said, "Do you see him?" "O yes!" she replied, "can't you?" and soon after, as her feet dipped still deeper into the river, she sweetly sang:

> "There is sweet rest in heaven."

Loved, gone from earth! Your memories we cherish. As thy life is, soon shall ours be; then, in one unbroken band, we'll sing Christ's power to save.

> "We have friends in spirit-land,
> Not shadows in a shadowy band;
> Not others, but themselves are they."

October 23*d.* Over a month since my last date. Has been a month, in some respects, of trial; in others, of joyful triumph through the blood of the Lamb. The candle of the Lord has shone upon my pathway with a steady light, cheering all the dark places. Am in a land of strangers.

> "A stranger in the world below,
> I calmly sojourn here;"

and yet I'm not a stranger. Every-where I go I find some of my Father's family. "Fellow-citizens with the saints, and of the household of God; made nigh by the blood of Christ."

Have just returned from our first quarterly-meeting; my first meeting with this people.

Went, trusting in the promise, "My grace is sufficient." The presence of God was felt among the people. While Brother G. was preaching, Sabbath morning, a number shouted aloud. Sabbath evening, God's blessing again rested upon his people. The glory of the Lord filled the house. My soul drank from the fountain until the small earthly vessel could contain no more, and I gave vent to the joy within in praises to Jesus.

The adversary afterward suggested that it would have been better not to have made quite so public a demonstration while so perfectly a stranger; but the earnest desire of my soul replied, "Let not only my lips, but my *life*, with all its powers, be employed in spreading Thy praise abroad." My soul was exceedingly happy during the night. Never in my life have I felt more like giving myself to the work than at present.

January 24, 1866. The labors of another year are entered upon. Its first hour found me renewing my covenant with God; "by the mercies of God" presenting my body "a living sacrifice." The altar is Christ. There my offering is this morning. The eternal Word is my refuge. On its promises I stand. My feet are pressing solid rock! Alleluiah!

At present, am with father at F., where, with

many discouragements, he is engaged in laboring for the salvation of souls. Lord, revive thy work!"

Last evening was the fourth I have been here, and the first in which any female but myself took a part; but with a Wesley, I am ready to say, "Let me stand single and alone, if need be." But, O Father, raise up here, for thine own sake, witnesses for Christ!

When, O when, shall the cry of God's Israel be, "For Zion's sake will I not hold my peace, and for Jerusalem's sake I will not rest, until the righteousness thereof go forth as brightness, and the salvation thereof as a lamp that burneth?" Then, and not until then, will our beloved Zion "stand forth as the morning, fair as the moon, clear as the sun, and terrible as an army with banners."

The great want of the Church at the present age, is earnest workers—men and women everywhere baptized with power from on high, who are ready for any work, the "child-work" and "man-work;" who dare, as one has it, to give to the Church "all the God-talk in them, without changing an accent;" those who on their breastplate will ever bear the motto, "Victory or death," and who are ready unflinchingly to carry the blood-stained banner of the Cross into the ranks of the enemy.

Were the Church, with her millions, such an army, where is the power that could stand before her? May the day hasten when she shall thus, all over our land, put on her strength, her beautiful array!

January 26th. Yesterday was spent with father in calling from house to house. Last evening was a precious season to my soul. I arose in the congregation to witness for Christ, and the power of the Highest rested upon me, and I felt that, had there been present a congregated world, undaunted I could have told them of the love of Jesus. I almost forgot that I was still a resident of earth, so near seemed the heavenly world, while the glory within inspired this poor, lisping, stammering tongue.

> "The Church triumphant in thy love,
> Their mighty joys we know;
> They sing the Lamb in hymns above,
> And we in hymns below."

The Church seems in a degree reviving; but O, what need of a thorough work! There is much feeling among the unconverted. To-morrow is our quarterly-meeting at W. May the Savior be with us!

January 29th. Again at F., where we came last evening after our quarterly-meeting services.

The Lord was with his people. Felt in the lovefeast to praise God that my lot has been cast for a season with this dear people.

> "Surely Thou didst unite
> Our kindred spirits here,
> That all hereafter might
> Before thy throne appear."

One incident of the meeting made it a season ever to be remembered by me. My Ellen R., two years ago this Winter, though not then eight years of age, gave good evidence of a change of heart, and was taken within the folds of the Church. The news of her conversion reached her dear father but a few days before his triumphant discharge from the Church below, and welcome to the Church above. In reference to her, he wrote: "I had rather my children would be *early* seekers of the 'pearl of great price,' become *early* the subjects of saving grace, than to have them become possessors of the accumulated wealth of a universe, or of the highest honors earth can boast." And all through that *last* letter were written exclamations of joy and praise for God's mercy in answer to prayer, manifested in the conversion of his little E.

She is possessed, naturally, of a very timid, shrinking nature, and though oft found in secret upon her knees, and often, of her own accord, collecting her young playmates together for a prayer-meeting, from which she would come with her face beaming with the love of Christ,—yet would often burst into tears as the public cross was from time to time presented. On yesterday she, unsolicited—though the church was crowded—arose in love-feast, and told in her child-like way, but in a manner which touched every heart, of the love of Jesus; and at the sacrament arose, and kneeled alone at the altar, and received at the hands of brother P. the emblems of the dying love of Christ, who, when upon earth, took little children in his arms, and blessed them; while the exclamation of, "Children have the best right to come," and the tearful eyes of the congregation, assured my heart that no one there was disposed to forbid her.

Who will say that the spirit of that departed father hovered not over that child as she there commemorated the sufferings of her dying Savior? Again to me seemed echoed from that Richmond hospital, "Tell my family to meet me in heaven." To-day my heart responds, "We are coming." Together we will by and by sit down at the marriage-supper of the Lamb; and for the accomplishment of this, "Thy will be done." Yea: rather let this heart break in its anguish here, than that we be there a divided band.

January 31*st.* The Lord is with us, speaking through lips of humble clay, and hearts of adamant are being broken. Some are coming to Christ.

Last evening, went to the house of prayer with so great a burden of soul that it seemed insupportable. Father preached from, "What shall it profit a man, if he shall gain the whole world and lose his own soul?" Unusual solemnity rested upon the congregation. It almost seemed that, for a time, the curtain hiding the realities of the other world was drawn aside, while we gazed upon the joys of the saved and the miseries of the lost.

The call for seekers was made; but no one moved. Then the Church were invited forward to seek a deeper baptism of power from on high. I arose to go, but so clearly did I feel that decisions were being made for eternity, and that to-morrow it might be too late for some present to make their peace with Heaven, that I turned to the brethren and sisters and told them that I felt I could not go to the altar without some of my unconverted friends with me; and then, drawn by a power almost irresistible, went to the back part of the congregation, and with tears and entreaties invited them separately and collectively to come to Christ. Some wept aloud, but did not move; and at their feet I bowed, and pleaded with the insulted Spirit in their behalf.

The spirit of entreaty and exhortation rested upon the Church; and, with earnest pleadings, they besought the unsaved to be reconciled to God. If they refuse, some of us feel that their blood will not be found upon our skirts. I tremble for the results of this day. Decisions are being made that will tell upon the eternal destiny of souls.

May 11*th.* Seasons of interest, precious seasons, have passed since a record has here been made; but indelibly are they written upon memory's tablet, and in eternity they will not be forgotten. Trials have been mine until my soul has cried out, "All thy waves and thy billows are gone over me." But my soul has rested upon the word, "I will be with him in trouble: I will deliver him, and honor him."

Never before have I so fully realized the blessedness of the eternal truth, "And we know that all things work"—not shall work, but—"work together for good to them that love God." The trials of earth are bringing me nearer thee, O precious Savior!

"By the thorn road, and none other,
Is the mount of vision won."

It's the path my Savior trod before me, and I'll press on. My soul exclaims, "Pure and spotless let me be!" 'Mid the fiery trials of earth, let me but, like Moses' bush, "mount the higher," and "flourish unconsumed in fire," and I'm content!

Two years to-day since my companion fell a sacrifice upon the altar of his country. Two years has he been singing the song of the redeemed. Long and weary ones, O my Truman! have they been to her thou hast left behind to battle alone against sin; but were they ten thousand instead, to thee it were happiness, eternity but just begun. I leave thee with Him who gave thee such victory, such peace to bear with thee above. We are not a separated family! I claim the sentiment of a sainted Wesley:

> "One family we dwell in Him,
> One Church above, beneath,
> Though now divided by the stream,
> The narrow stream, of death."

THE CHRISTIAN'S LEGACY.

"For unto you it is given, in behalf of Christ, not only to believe on him, but also to suffer for his sake."

A love of suffering, for its own sake, can never be. Every law of our nature shrinks from the fiery ordeal, either of body or mind; but Eternal Wisdom hath chosen that through suffering the graces of the Christian should be brought to a state of perfection which no other means can accomplish. And shall finite man, all ignorance and blindness, cry out against the process by which his prayer, "Create in me a clean heart, O God!" is being answered? Shall the clay say to the potter, "Why hast thou formed me thus?" Rather, let the cry of the heart be:

> "Deepen the wound thy hands have made
> In this weak, helpless soul,
> Till mercy, with its balmy aid,
> Descend to make me whole.
>
> The sharpness of thy two-edg'd sword
> Enable me to endure,
> Till bold to say my hall'wing Lord
> Hath wrought a perfect cure."

And then, when, in answer to this prayer, the chastening hand of God is laid upon us, let us glorify God that unto us "it is given, in behalf of Christ, not only to believe in him, but also to suffer for his sake."

Shall we ask for the pure gold, for the dross of our nature to be destroyed, and then murmur at the refining process? Shall we ask for the white raiment wherewith to be clothed, and then contend with him who washeth whiter than snow?

Years since, in the beginning of a walk of faith—all ignorance in regard to the way, but a babe beginning to walk while our mind was in a state of wonderment and perplexity, suffering intensely from the buffetings of Satan and from surrounding circumstances, yet endeavoring to hold fast our integrity—we bowed at the throne of grace, earnestly pleading for DELIVERANCE; but it came not. We opened the Word of God, seeking there for comfort and deliverance. The eye rested upon, "Beloved, think it not strange concerning the fiery trial which is to try you, as though some strange thing happened unto you; but rejoice, inasmuch as ye are partakers of Christ's sufferings; that when his glory shall be revealed, ye may be glad also with exceeding joy."

From that hour, how precious the exhortation! Faith in the eternal Word enabled us to receive it as spoken from the throne, fully believing and resting upon the Word, "that the trial of your faith being much more precious than of gold that perisheth, THOUGH IT BE TRIED WITH FIRE, might be found unto praise and honor and glory at the appearing of Christ, whom, not having seen, ye love; in whom, though now ye see him not, yet believing, ye rejoice with joy unspeakable and full of glory, receiving the end of your faith, even the salvation of your souls."

Years have since passed by; but this legacy—to suffer—is still mine. The oft-repeated prayer, "Nearer, my God, to thee," has entered the ear of the Most High. That prayer is being answered; but in answering, "He hath led me by a way which I knew not."

The storms of earth are passing, and I am nearing HOME. Already, at times, I seem to catch glimpses of the snowy robes of loved ones passed over—of *one* dearer to me than life itself, whose body, in a far-off, unknown grave, is moldering back to dust; but while, as ever and anon borne on the breeze from that soldier's grave, comes the soothing murmur, "Not here, but risen," re-echoed by, "Jesus said unto her, I am the resurrection and the life," we look up, knowing the loved of earth are placed on the evergreen shore to bring us nearer God and heaven; and with rapture, our soul triumphantly exclaims:

> "I know I am nearing the holy ranks
> Of friends and kindred dear.
>
> I've almost gained my heavenly home;
> My spirit loudly sings;
> The holy ones, behold they come!
> I hear the noise of wings;"

then come down from Pisgah's mount, and join with the few who in spirit sing:

> "The cross for Christ I'll cherish,
> Its crucifixion bear;

> All hail reproach or sorrow,
> If Jesus lead me there!"

I wait the resurrection morn for the knowledge of the whys and wherefores. Now, as from God himself, we hear the words sounding, reverberating in the magnitude of their meaning, "The just shall live by faith."

Dear reader, have the storms of earth reached thy dwelling, threatening to ingulf thy frail bark? Look up! List for the voice, and above the foam-capped billow thou shalt hear, "Peace, be still!"

Firmer and firmer let us cling to the vine; and by and by, from our resting-place on the Rock, forever we shall look down on rocks that threaten and waves that o'erwhelm the soul no more. Until then, look for fragrance to come from the wounded part; look amid thy sorrows for the touch of Him who turneth darkness into day; for true it is, that

> "Sorrow, touched by Him, grows bright
> With more than rapture's ray;
> As darkness shows us worlds of light
> We never saw by day."

Grace comes as often to us clad in the dark robes of affliction as in more shining attire. "What are these which are arrayed in white robes, and whence came they?" Listen to the answer: " These are they which came out of great tribulation, and have washed their robes and made them white in the blood of the Lamb. Therefore are they before the throne." May God inspire our hearts with the laudable desire to get near the throne!

CHAPTER V.

JUNE 28TH. Would that earth had language in which to speak satisfactorily of the precious seasons I have been permitted to enjoy since my last date! But O, how incompetent am I to tell of the joys of the redeemed! My soul reaches forward to know more of Christ. Shall it ever be satisfied? Thank God, the answer we find in the Word which abideth forever: "I shall be satisfied when I awake with Thy likeness."

> " Far out of sight, while yet the flesh enfolds us,
>   Lies the fair country where our hearts abide;
> And of its bliss is nought more wondrous told us
>   Than these few words, " I shall be satisfied."

Yet earth has its seasons, while in communion with God's people, when the soul, drinking so freely of the streams which make glad the city of our God, seemingly could endure no more, and not escape from its prison-house and soar away to join the blood-washed above.

Such a season was our

ALBION CAMP-MEETING.

Here we were privileged to sit, for the first time, under the teachings of Doctor and Mrs. Palmer. O, how many went from that meeting impressed, as never before, with the truth, " Holiness is power!" And with this newly-found power, many, we may hope, went to raise the "banner of holiness;" and many who had been tremblingly raising the standard, went to their fields of labor to raise it higher.

Other banners, stained with sin, were trampled in the dust while with these Fletchers of our day we joined in singing:

" O, who'll stand up for Jesus,
   The lowly Nazarene?
And raise the blood-stained banner
Amid the hosts of sin?"

The hasty visit of Doctor and Mrs. Palmer to our state was to not a few an epoch in our life-history. Said many—some of them God's honored legates of the skies—"I see the way of faith as never before, its simplicity, its power;" and we all went from that grove meeting, feeling, as said our beloved presiding elder in our closing love-feast after their departure, that their visit to us had been "as the visit of angels." A hundred, it was estimated, were brought to Christ, and as many more fully saved. To God be all the glory!

This was our centenary convening, in this part of our state. Thought was turned to the past of the history of Methodism in our lovely West. Never was there a more perfect fulfillment of the prophecy: "The wilderness and the solitary place shall be glad for them; and the desert shall rejoice and blossom as the rose. It shall blossom abundantly, and rejoice even with joy and singing." The memory of the "just is blessed." Thus is the memory of those who, during the past century, have, sowing beside all waters, toiled in our midst. They labored when small and feeble was the day, and have gone up to receive their reward. We, above their sacred ashes, sing:

"See how great a flame aspires,
Kindled by a spark of grace!"

Thank God! The Word doth "swiftly run." We now hear the shout from the mountains of the far West, and the vales and valleys echo back in joyful reply: "A WAY IS HERE! It is called the way of holiness."

We are not left in sadness to sing of former days better than these, but with joy we behold Zion coming up out of the wilderness, leaning upon her beloved, and with the Psalmist we exclaim, "Out of Zion the perfection of beauty, God hath shined;" and, "Beautiful for situation, the joy of the whole earth, is Mount Zion." Tried long in the furnace, 't is true; but she flourishes still, unconsumed in fire, and hastening to attire herself in her bridal array. Already the exultant strain has commenced: " I will greatly rejoice in the Lord: my soul shall be joyful in my God; for he hath clothed me with the garments of salvation; he hath covered me with the robe of righteousness as a bridegroom decketh himself with ornaments, and as a bride adorneth herself with her jewels."

In looking upon the past and present of our beloved Zion, may not we expect glorious things in the future? The army of Christ in all the different branches of the Church is steadily increasing; and though, for over eighteen hundred years, all the combined powers of darkness have been brought to bear against it, offensive in her movements she stands to-day, "Onward," the motto, while on the banner unfurled to the breezes that float from Calvary we read, "Victory through the blood of the Lamb!" God be praised that the spirit of the martyrs is with us still! Men and women there are, scattered here and there, all over our land, who, with the standard of holiness firmly planted, are ready at the command of our Captain to push the battle to the very gate of the enemy—who, at every call of the Master, are responding, "Here am I; send me."

Beholding by faith the eternal triumph of our holy Christianity, knowing that

> "Jesus shall reign where'er the sun
> Does his successive journeys run,"

onward they move; and we, catching the exultant strains of their music rising above the mists of unbelief, with triumph join their song:

> "Thy saints in all this glorious war
> Shall conquer, though they die;
> They see the triumph from afar—
> By faith they bring it nigh."

O, the power of holiness—of a life of faith! May this way—the simple, royal way of faith and obedience—speedily spread all over our Western States, until Jesus' love the whole land shall fire, and "set the kingdoms on a blaze!"

July 1st. Am again with my beloved sisters at Coldwater. The tie binding our hearts by this meeting is being strengthened. Last Friday was a day never to be forgotten by us, for its earnest struggle of soul for our approaching feast of tabernacles on Coldwater District, and for

THE VICTORY GAINED.

IT was the sacred hour of prayer—an hour set apart by a few made one in Christ, separated in the flesh, in which to meet each other around one common mercy-seat, and mingle their voices at the throne of grace, for the promotion of holiness in their own hearts and that of brethren and sisters in Christ.

In the providence of God, after having been long separated, three of the little band had met. Preparations were being made to meet God's Israel in the tented grove. The day had been set apart as one of fasting and prayer, in which to present "large petitions to a King" for the salvation of God to rest upon his people while on the encampment. The soul had prepared its suit, fully believing that "Jesus loves to answer prayer."

Years before, the injunction had been obeyed by these now bold ones in Christ, "I beseech you therefore, brethren, by the mercies of God, that ye present your bodies a living sacrifice, holy, acceptable unto God, which is your reasonable service." And now the cry of these earnest hearts was not only to be presented spotless before the throne, but that the "whole spirit and soul and body be preserved blameless unto the coming of our Lord Jesus Christ."

It was an hour of deep heart-searching. The sharpness of the two-edged sword was being endured. Duties crossing to nature were being presented, and glorious results from these were looming up.

It had been asked that God's people might be so endued with power from on high to do battle for the Lord, might be so enabled to carry the banner of "Holiness unto the Lord," shouting, "Victory through the blood of the Lamb!" as to scatter confusion amid the ranks of the enemy. Petition after petition was being presented, tending directly to the results of the coming week's stay in the wilderness.

Faith was grasping the desired blessings for the glory of God alone. 'T was laughing at impossibilities, and crying, "It shall be done." The flesh, which cries out, "It can not be," was silence keeping before the Lord.

Already faith, grasping the unseen, was beholding God's embassadors upon the walls of Zion, speaking with the anointing that abideth; the Church arising, "her light being come;" the Spirit speaking through lips of humble clay,— while hearts of stone were breaking, and rebels were being brought at the feet of Sovereign Mercy.

But list! what cometh here? Ah! the regions of darkness are alarmed, and in commotion. An embassador is sent. With fiendish purposes, he mingles with soft whispers in that little group. Shall he prevail? Too well are the insinuations of the tempter interpreted! The name of his Conqueror is repeated: "Victory through Immanuel! Glory to Jesus!" With disappointment he quits the field, and Israel gains the day. With conquered mien, he returns to his dark abode. Hell is in mourning.

Long these victorious ones continue in praise to their Conquering King. Joyfully they sing:

> "Angels now are hovering round us,
> Unperceived amid the throng,
> Wondering at the love that crowned us,
> Glad to join the holy song."

The Spirit taketh of the "things of God and revealeth them unto babes;" and, strong in the strength which God supplies through his eternal Son, they go out from that hour's contest to become henceforth not only defensive in standing against the assaults of the arch-deceiver, but offensive in their movements, attacking the seemingly strong fortifications of the enemy, with the standard of holiness lifted higher than before, carrying the blood-stained banner of the cross even amid the hosts of sin.

Was there no victory in this unseen contest, no ground gained? It will never be sounded to the eager, excitement-loving world as a "glorious victory;" but by and by, in the great summary, it will be known who is the greatest conqueror: he that subdues a world and brings it in subjection at his feet, or he that "overcometh" and is made "a pillar in the temple of God;" who goeth "no more out;" upon whom is written "the name of God, and the name of the city of my God, which is New Jerusalem," and to whom shall finally be given the inheritance, "To him that overcometh will I grant to sit with me on my throne, even as I also overcame and am sit down with my Father on his throne."

> "Angels our march oppose,
>   Who still in strength excel,
> Our secret, sworn, eternal foes,
>   Countless, invisible.
> From thrones of glory driven,
>   By flaming vengeance hurled,
> They throng the air, and darken heaven,
>   And rule this lower world.
>
> But shall believers fear?
>   But shall believers fly?
> Or see the bloody cross appear,
>   And all their powers defy?
> By all hell's host withstood,
>   We all hell's host o'erthrow;
> And, conquering them through Jesus' blood,
>   We on to conquer go."

July 2d. Yesterday, after services which were so precious to our souls while we sat together in the sanctuary, I went with sister C. to the home of our dear sister T., to spend the remainder of the day in social prayer and converse of the deep things of God; and together we again "sat in an heavenly place in Christ Jesus."

Never did heaven and earth seem more completely blended into one than on that Sabbath afternoon, as we three communed at the blood-bought mercy-seat. Again it was, *ask* and *receive*. My soul is filled with wonder at the condescension of the King of kings and Lord of lords. "Whosoever will do the will of my Father which is in heaven, the same is my brother and sister and mother."

July 11*th*. Have just come from the tented grove. O, how gloriously have we been permitted to realize the victories gained on that memorable Friday!

Nearly every charge on the district was represented by some, strong in the strength of Israel's God, ready to do battle for the Lord. God's chosen embassadors spoke with lips touched anew with living coals from off the altar, until, in wonder, many exclaimed, "We never saw it in this wise!"

Battle after battle was fought, until near two

hundred, in answer to the prayer, labor, and united faith of the Church, had brought their weapons of warfare and laid them at the feet of their Conquering King. Many sought and obtained the blessing of purity, the baptism of the Holy Ghost, the tongue of fire.

GIFT OF POWER RECEIVED.

REV. G. NEWTON, one of the Lord's chosen watchmen, from an adjoining state, came, earnestly seeking, as he expressed it, "the gift of power," some overwhelming manifestation while in the wilderness. He had previously entered the rest of faith; but desired *power to labor*, to lead on his people to the immediate possession of

> "The land of rest from inbred sin,
> The land of perfect holiness."

The gift of power was given; but not as expected. The way was clearly presented (as he since writes), that all needful power to glorify God would be given as needed, so long as he moved forward in careful obedience to the Spirit's voice; and by faith he sweetly rested in the assurance that, as his day so would his strength be.

Before leaving the ground (on Friday), he had asked the prayers of two interested ones, especially for Sabbath evening. Of this he writes:

"I was looking for victory; I expected it. I knew you prayed for me. But O, what a struggle I had amidst thick darkness before evening service! My body, weak and faint, invited Satan's attack. But I had learned to walk by faith, seeing the Invisible One by my side, though greatly pressed. Night came; larger congregation than usual; and, from stepping into the pulpit, power was given. God was manifest to mortal sense. The opening prayer led near the Throne! My soul seemed burdened for the Church, and, taking a text the Spirit had led me to in answer to prayer (Isaiah lxvi, 4), I portrayed the state of Israel's backslidden children, and that God would not always be trifled with, but will visit their fears upon them with an awful realization. The Lord blessed, and, at its close, I called all who would ask the baptism of the Spirit to surround the altar. I never saw such a readiness; and, as we poured out our souls in prayer, blessings came, and I realized *victory* had been given.

"Monday, I was led to pray that my body might be sustained, as it generally, in that day, has subjected me to fierce temptations; and it was!

"But whilst I have precious victories, I have severe struggles. Last evening, at another point on my charge, at a prayer-meeting, several souls were blessed with pardon, and others are praying for purity. Even in July, a revival of religion is in waiting for us here."

Was permitted here to form many new associations, which will be lasting as eternity itself. O, ye dear ones in Christ, with whom I've met and parted! How strong the tie binding my heart to yours. We may never meet again on earth; never here again unite in songs of praise and mingled vows, which have made our communion so sweet; but up yonder in our Father's mansion, we shall surely meet.

> "O, what a joyful meeting there!
> In robes of white array'd;
> Palms in our hands we all shall bear,
> And crowns upon our head."

We shall know each other there, as here, and together we'll walk—not earth's paths of sorrow—but the gold-paved streets of the New Jerusalem; for heaven's gate shall surely, if we are but faithful a few days longer, open for us, as one after another we sleep in Jesus.

The fellowship of souls made one in Christ, *here*, is, beyond expression, precious; but how much more glorious when, with the Church, redeemed from all iniquity, free from every spot and wrinkle! The fellowship of saints will then be made known as on earth it can not be; and, O my Father, may I be one!

> "O, let my lot be cast with these,
> The least of Jesus' witnesses;
> O, that my Lord would count me meet
> To wash his dear disciples' feet!"

August 1st. Am now at my present home at W.; the aim and happiness of my life "to glorify God, and enjoy him forever." Spend some time in writing. Has been something of a trial to find my name with what, a short time since, was written for the "Guide and Beauty." It is what I never intended. I shrink from thus being exposed to the view of thousands; but God's will be done. Perhaps this is one of the ways in which I am to bind my offering upon the altar. While so great a number of witnesses hold me in full survey, the Lord help me to run well, even unto the end! O, how weak human endeavors, human reliances! Were these my trust, I were undone; but my weakness with "Thy strength" I join. THAT STRENGTH shall enable me to trample beneath my feet my foes, and, following my Guide, on to conquest go.

August 21st. God is still dealing most graciously with my soul. Have an intense desire to tell a world what a dear Savior I have found; for the arms of love that are encompassing me would embrace all mankind. Feel oft, as did a sainted Fletcher, "O, for a gust of praise to go through the breadth and length of our land!"

Was permitted, last week, to meet with God's people on the Ann-Arbor Camp-ground. Was a stranger among that people, but the language they spoke I knew; the songs they sang were those of Zion, and very soon I could but exclaim, we are "no more strangers and foreigners," but are "made nigh by the blood of Christ." The spirit of prayer in which I went, was to be enabled to get more entirely out of self into Christ, and to this prayer I realized an answer.

On Wednesday evening of this meeting, after services at the stand were closed, while engaged in social prayer at the family altar, while asking that the "banner of holiness might be lifted on the ground, as it had not yet been," suddenly the whole encampment seemed enveloped in a glorious light, and so distinct, to my vision, was this light, that I as suddenly fell to the ground as if struck by lightning. It was but for the moment, as I immediately had power to arise again. A Divine influence pervaded the entire encampment. Our tent seemed filled with the glory of God. Some shouted aloud; while others seemed filled with silent awe. All spoke afterward of the influence in the tent and about the ground as being sudden and overpowering.

Thursday, Doctor and Mrs. Palmer came upon the ground, and with them I was permitted to enjoy most precious seasons of communion, both at public exercises and in private conversation. Mrs. Palmer said many things to me which will always be remembered; among these, that I must "forever settle in my mind that when, for the Divine glory, I asked help of the Spirit, and obediently went forward, that help WAS given;" also, that I was "too much inclined to question in regard to the performance of public duty;" and that I must "ask of the Lord a stronger voice for those duties;" to which I could respond, "Just what shall be most for Thy glory I dare ask of thee." Find my soul so fully in sympathy with Christ in the great work of saving a world, that no sacrifice I can make in this work seems too great; and the grace of God, his love constraining, inspiring me, is overcoming the natural timidity and shrinkings of nature, and enabling me joyfully to go forward, glorying in nothing save the cross. O, the cross! How it has subdued the pride of this heart!

"It makes the coward spirit brave,
And nerves the feeble arm for fight;

> It takes the terror from the grave,
> And gilds the bed of death with light."

Here the heart's best affections do, and shall forever, cluster; and with the cross my strength, lead where thou wilt, O Redeemer! I'll follow thee. The Lord enable me to help raise the standard of holiness to his glory. I love this banner; the banner committed to us as a people, that it might "be displayed because of the truth;" but O, how many of our leaders in Zion permit it to droop! But God be praised that some of the watchmen do give the certain sound. Some do prove their high commission by being

> "Temples of the Holy Ghost,
> And fill'd with faith and hope and love."

"HE SET A CHILD IN THE MIDST."

AT this meeting, one evening, were bowed many who, with uplifted heart, were saying, "I would see Jesus;" some asking forgiveness for sins, the accumulation of years of wanderings; some seeking the spotless robe of Christ's righteousness, the beauty of saints; all alike dependent alone upon the merits of the Crucified. We kneeled by one of tender age, apparently not more than ten years, and asked, "For what have you come, my dear?" "For a clean heart," she replied, with a sweetness of manner we shall never forget.

By a few words of questioning, we found that, over a year previous, angels had carried the tidings home of this child saved from the dominion of sin, and a name had been registered in the Lamb's Book of Life ; and now, knowing that her Redeemer liveth, she had come seeking the beautiful dress without "spot or wrinkle or any such thing."

We remembered the words of the Savior, "Whoso shall offend one of these little ones which believe in me, it were better for him that a millstone were hanged about his neck and that he were drowned in the depth of the sea," and tried in simplicity to lead her to the open fountain ; and while Dr. and Mrs. P., who were present, sang,

"My sins are washed away
In the blood of the Lamb,"

an entire change came over her countenance. The large tears, which were forcing themselves down her face, seemed stayed in their course ; and, with a countenance radiant with joy, she arose to her feet, and, with clasped hands, stood, seemingly lost to all around, while the inner eye was with rapture fixed upon the "beauty of holiness."

Opportunity was given for testimony. With majestic calmness she said : "I love Jesus. He has given me a clean heart; has washed my sins away in his own blood." Who of that crowded altar doubted it? O, how we longed, as we stood there looking upon that lovely face, those clean, white robes of that child, to show her to every infidel, every unbelieving man or woman in our land! Methinks it would have been an argument unanswerable.

Thus shall the Church be, when clothed with her power, "holiness."

"Except ye be converted and become as little children, ye shall not enter the kingdom of heaven," was for hours after in our mind. "These things" are hid from the "wise and prudent," and revealed "unto babes."

May our Father in heaven save the Church from her vain philosophy and reasoning, and give her child-faith and simplicity!

CHAPTER VI.

PREPARED.

"Is that a death-bed where the Christian lies?
Yes: but not his. 'T is death itself there dies."

THIS, well has one said, is the land of the dying; yonder, the land of the living. What! call those dead who, with God's seal, "THEY ARE MINE," upon their brow, have walked amid earth's pollutions with garments white, overcoming through the blood of the Lamb — who have met the last foe, trampled his power beneath their feet, and, with shouts of victory, gone to be forever with the Lord!

"Who are these arrayed in white,
Brighter than the noonday sun,
Foremost of the sons of light,
Nearest the eternal throne?"

These are they we miss so much here. But our tears cease to flow; for we know their day has but just commenced; their sun risen, not set; theirs not an ended life, but one just begun.

O, happy they who have thus forever escaped from the land of the dying! And soon, our conflicts, our toils ended, we shall join them— not they come to us. O no: we would not have it thus; we shall go to them.

With such joyous thoughts, memory places oft before us the form of our beloved Mary,* an only daughter, possessed in a high degree of an amiableness of disposition and those adornments of nature which make life lovely.

At the age of thirteen, she gave her heart to God her Savior, and became henceforth an ornament to the Christian religion. Of none, perhaps, could it be more truly said, while for a few years she tarried in the Church militant, " His seal was on thy brow."

The first labor of this saved one was to induce her father to erect the family altar; nor could she be persuaded to retire for the night until the desire of her heart was granted. This earnestness characterized her future labors. Love being the motive power, no obstacle thrown in the way of her onward progress was too great to be surmounted; seeking not, like some who have taken upon them the name of a follower of the Lamb, to see how near the pit of perdition they may drive their chariot-wheels, and yet finally be

* Miss M. L. Smith.

admitted at heaven's gate, but how near heaven she might live here; searching God's Word, as for hidden treasure, to find the narrow way.

At the age of eighteen, she received Christ, an all-sufficient Savior, joyful to find the way so beautifully described by the prophet: "A way shall be there, and a highway. It shall be called the way of holiness."

From this time, the nobleness of the victory that overcometh the world, even our faith, was exemplified in the life of Mary. Possessed of a reserved and shrinking nature, grace overcoming the fear of man, glorying in the cross was the more manifest; and she was permitted to know, even before the spirit burst its house of clay, that her labor was not in vain in the Lord. Hers· we know, though but few years were given in which to win souls, is no starless crown.

We love to remember the "enduring" in hours of darkness, "as seeing Him who is invisible," the triumph in Christ as she went from strength to strength; but there is a scene that we always feel was

> "Privileged beyond the common walks
> Of virtuous life, quite on the verge of heaven."

It is where our loved Mary passed up from the Church below to the Church above. Heaven has always seemed nearer since with her we went down to the brink of the river, saw her fearless plunge, and caught the echoes of the music on the other side, as the white-robed company welcomed her home.

Her final illness lasted some five days, during which she suffered beyond expression; but, when permitted a season of comparative ease, her favorite expressions were, "My father's at the helm; my Jesus doeth all things well."

A few hours before her death, she called a dear aunt to her bedside, and asked her opinion in regard to her recovery. On being told that she had no evidence in respect to her restoration to health, she replied, "I have no choice."

Soon after, being taken violently worse, the physician pronounced her dying; but, as soon as she could speak, she exclaimed, with all the earnestness of which she was capable, "Christians, live! Christians, live!" and, with sentences of earnest entreaty and warning, exhorted those present to be faithful in the service of Christ.

To her mother, whom she sought to comfort, she said, "Go to Jesus with all your sorrows; he'll help you every time." To her father, for whom she had long prayed, desiring to see him take a decided stand for Christ, "You know the way;" then gave her Bible to her brother of twelve years of age, and held his hand until he promised to meet her in heaven. To her betrothed she said, "We shall soon meet in that better land;" then said to her aunt, "Sing," and joined her in singing several hymns; then requested her to pray, and, when she ceased, broke out in prayer herself.

Her countenance now beamed with unearthly radiance; and, to those who looked on and listened to her words, she seemed no longer like an inhabitant of earth.

After praying for friends, the neighborhood, her brethren and sisters in Christ, she asked that the place might be made holy ground; and for herself, as her last earthly boon, "perfect victory in death." God was very near, and quickly answered the petition; and she shouted aloud the praises of her Redeemer until her strength was exhausted.

Soon after, the adversary, unwilling that such complete triumph should be hers, suggested, "You asked this blessing to be seen of men." She mentioned it to one standing by, who replied: "Mary, that was the tempter. Put your trust in God." She immediately replied, "Though he slay me, yet will I trust in him."

This was the last conflict, after which she

conversed but little, exclaiming oft, in prayer, "Jesus, come a little nearer!" and to those around: "'T is nothing to die. Jesus is here."

After the physicians present had pronounced her nearly gone, she requested her pastor, Rev. Wm. Birdsall, to sing, and joined him in singing:

"We're going home, to die no more."

But the chariot was waiting; and, lifting up her hands in token of victory, she exclaimed, "Though I walk through the valley of the shadow of death, I will fear no evil; for thou art with me: thy rod and thy staff they comfort me;" and was borne by her heavenly escort to her home above.

We've laid the form of our loved one in the tomb, but we know she is not there. By faith, we behold her mingling with the blood-washed around the throne. Sometimes we almost apprehend her presence here, and list to hear her softly whisper words of holy triumph as before; and she seems beckoning us upward, where friends never part.

"The sting of death is sin, and the strength of sin is the law: but thanks be unto God, which giveth us the victory through our Lord Jesus Christ."

"O, how wonderful to see
Death and life in conflict meet!

> Life hath won the victory,
> Trodden death beneath his feet."

And now we know that, to the Christian,

> "There is no death; what seems so is transition:
> This life of mortal breath
> Is but the suburb of the life Elysian,
> Whose portal we call death."

UNPREPARED.

WHAT a contrast to my meditations of yesterday! Have just come from the bedside of one with no hope of life beyond the grave—a young lady, possessed, as was our dear Mary, with all those surroundings that combine to make life useful and happy. But hers was the vain search for happiness in the world.

In the ball-room, 'mid the pleasure-loving throng, she sought to drown the gentle wooings of the Good Shepherd, who would fain have led her into green pastures, beside living waters. Friends had affectionately urged upon her his claims; but, "Not now," was her repeated reply.

Four weeks ago to-day, she stood at the altar, a happy bride; but the interests of the soul were still forgotten.

To-day, the cry was made: "Behold the Heavenly Bridegroom cometh!" "Go ye out to meet him!"

Friends gathered round, and told her of the summons, pointing her to the Lamb of God, who saved the thief upon the cross. But it was TOO LATE to make the needful preparations. In anguish she exclaimed, " O, I can not die! Do n't tell me I must die!" and then in unconsciousness passed through the dark valley.

> "How shocking was thy summons, O death,
> To her that was at ease in her possessions;
> Who, counting on long years of pleasure here,
> Was quite unfurnished for the world to come!"

In her bridal garments we dressed her for the tomb, while all the time the question was forcing itself upon our mind, "Will *this* bridal attire answer to appear in before the ' King of kings?'"

Our Bridegroom has provided the "white robes," and given the command, "Be ye also ready;" and who, without this attire, dare go out to meet him? O, who can bear the anger of an offended God?

Let me wear *here* the spotless robes of Christ's righteousness, watching ever for the coming of the Master!

> "There is a death whose pang
> Outlasts the fleeting breath;
> O, what eternal horrors hang
> Around the second death!"

September 1st. The Lord of Hosts again met his people in his own tabernacle (Moscow Camp-meeting), made without hands. Here the time was spent in united effort for the glory of God, with my dear friend, Mrs. M. H. Twogood. Why have our lots been cast together? Are we not made one in answer to Christ's own prayer for his disciples, "That they all may be one: as thou, Father, art in me and I in thee, that they also may be one in us: that the world may believe that thou hast sent me?"

We have drank of the same cup of bereavement, are alike in aims and aspirations, joys and sorrows, and more—are united in Christ by the band of love, the threefold cord which never can be broke.

This time was almost constantly occupied in labor for others, in which God greatly blessed. Some battles were fought and victories won. Thanks be unto God, who "always causeth us to triumph in Christ."

October 7th. Another conference year is commenced. Father is returned to W. and F. The toils, the battles, and, we trust, holy triumphs of another year, are before us. Already the battle has commenced. The adversary is busy; but we expect it will be seen that there is a God in Israel.

'T is Sabbath evening, the close of our first

quarterly-meeting. We have here many discouragements,—the greatest of them all, the coldness of the Church; the great want in some (and those our leaders in Zion), of the mind of Christ. O, how painful to see those who should be, and to whom we have a right to look, as lights spiritually, led by the great arch-deceiver! Were our trust in human help, we should surely fail; but looking to God alone, resting upon the firm foundation of his Word, "For in due season ye shall reap if ye faint not," we go forth "weeping," our record on high, proving the trial of our faith more precious than "of gold that perisheth."

There is a day of rest coming for the weary itinerant. How glorious then his triumph, carrying his sheaves with him!

Our hearts have been greatly cheered, of late, by the news of the conversion of a dear uncle, for whose salvation many prayers have been offered in the past. These prayers were answered in

EDDY'S MISSION.

UPON a mission on earth, bringing joy and sunshine, with little feet pattering from morn till night, and joyous laugh ringing every-where, came little Eddy, pet Eddy; while fond parents and three sisters clasped him tightly in their grasp of love. But a mission hast thou, darling boy, not only to bring joy and gladness, but to wring hearts with anguish. Why this?

In childish glee, he climbs upon the knee of one he loves, and, throwing his tiny arms around her neck, says:

"Grandma, Eddy's got wings growing."

"Hush, darling! Grandma will need wings first."

"Grandma will have big wings; but Eddy's 'most big enough now!"

In a few days, death opens the door for the "caged bird," and Eddy joins the warblers above. His body rests in a short, narrow bed in the city cemetery. His wings, if needed, have carried the spirit up to the bright Elysium.

From that hour of dark sorrow to those bereaved parents, that unconverted father hears ever a little voice, saying:

"Come this way, my father—
Steer straight for me;
Here, safe on the shore,
I am waiting for thee."

'T is the hour of worship. In a crowded city church a man of influence arises, and, with subdued utterance, speaks of the slighted opportunities of years; of the repeated grievings of the spirit of God; of the late, perhaps last call, in the removal of a cherished idol; and, with deep contrition, before that congregation, pledges the remainder of his life to the cause of Christ.

Strong men are touched, and weep; and, one after another, arise and pledge themselves to "go to their Father." Thus the work goes on, until a hundred, from a life of sin and wandering, have turned their feet unto the testimonies of the Lord.

Was Eddy's mission upon earth, though so short, a useless one? Will he have any stars in his crown? Mourners, weeping beside little mounds, listening in vain for the pattering of little feet, joyous prattling, look upward! List for the voice, and thou shalt hear it: "I am waiting for thee!" And the mission of thy now angel babe to bring thee nearer God and heaven, to link with golden chain thy spirit near the throne, shall not have been in vain. And when thy work is done, thy darling, with harp and crown, standing on the ever-green shore, shall welcome thee home.

CHAPTER VII.

REV. H. LAW.

OCTOBER 8TH. The news of battles fought and victories won have filled our land with rejoicing ; while long and continued have been the shouts echoing from north to south, and from east to west, of triumph over a vanquished foe. Of a greater, more glorious battle fought and victory won our pen to-day writes :

> " O, the burst gates, crushed sting, demolished throne,
> Last gasp of vanquished Death ! Shout earth and heaven !"

The particulars of the sudden death of Rev. H. Law, of the Michigan Conference, have just reached us. On Sabbath evening, September 9th, he went from his Conference, then in session at Hillsdale, to Mosherville, a previous field of labor, where he preached with unusual unction and power, from " Now, thanks be unto God, which always causeth us to triumph in Christ."

At the close he made an earnest and affecting appeal to the young people present, exhorting them to an immediate acquaintance with Christ; and then, with outspread arms, breathed forth the longings of his soul in "God bless this people!" and suddenly fell upon the altar near which he stood, shouting "Glory to God!" and "was not," for "God took him."

Brother Law was a holy man. What more can be said? Has fallen at his post; ceased at once to work and live. The startling and saddening news has been swiftly flying through our state, "Brother Law is dead!" This is the cry of mortals. Angels sing, and loud heaven echoes with their song, "HE LIVES!" By death he has only escaped from death, and immortality gained; his one desire on earth realized, "Forever with the Lord;" and, though his place is forever vacant on earth, long will he live in precious remembrances in the different charges and districts where he has labored.

Brother Law was dear to me—a friend in days of deep affliction. *They* have met in that better land, where sorrow is a word unknown, while sister Law and I *alone* journey thitherward; but there is to us whispering a voice which we know to be that of our God,

"I love thee! I love thee! pass under the rod!"

and the chain which death has broken in twain is being fastened still firmer to the skies.

Sister Law is being sustained to the glory of God's grace in this hour of bereavement. She thus writes me:

"*You* KNOW of the sorrow of hours like these. But the Lord is wonderfully sustaining me; and, though my heart has been riven as never before, the Savior has been so preciously near, and sometimes I have had so sweet an earnest of the glorious rest, that my sorrow has melted away in the blessed sunlight of the better clime.

"The Lord has been preparing me for weeks for this trial. I have had glorious victories; such pantings after God, such consecration, such pure, ardent love for the cause of Christ, I had never known before. But I need it all. I had been praying that my dear, precious husband might do more good this year than ever before in any of his life. I asked, with tearful pleadings, '*Anywhere, any sacrifice,*' so God might be honored, souls saved. The Lord heard my prayer; he answered, O how mysteriously! But I knew it was the twofold answer to *our* prayers. When they lifted his bowed form from the altar, the whole truth was plain from the first look. I said, 'It is the answer to his oft-made prayer, that he might go from labor to rest;' and in his thus going, I knew, was the answer to mine. Words can not express the feelings of my heart in this glorious hour, for it was heavenly. I had never heard him so clearly portray the triumphs of the Gospel as at this time; and to see him thus triumph over death with the waving of his hand, and a 'Glory be to God' upon his lips, was glorious.

"He was gone as soon as the ebbing blood could cease to flow—gone to his reward. I kneeled near him, to commend to God my interests and say, 'Thy will be done;' to know that my consecration was perfect, now so suddenly tested. The first words that escaped my lips were the last that fell from his, 'Glory be to God!' O, the victories of that hour! Earth faded; sorrow melted; heaven and earth strangely commingled, while with shouts of victory I joined with the redeemed around the throne, 'Unto Him who hath loved us and washed us in his own blood!'

"Heaven came to earth—earth rose to heaven. At times, the waves of sorrow pass over my soul, and if Jesus did not come quickly to strengthen, I could not endure it. This holy Sabbath morning I missed him so much! The books were ready for prayer. It seemed, for the moment, I must hear HIS voice. I could not see the words, and gave the book to Sister Caroline.

"No need, now, of the clean linen. No: for they are always clean and white. No need now to pray that physical strength may be given, the Holy Spirit's power imparted, that another Sabbath's labor may be done to the glory of God; for he 'rests from his labors,' and his 'works do follow him.'

> "'Father, to us vouchsafe the grace
>   Which brought our friend victorious through;
> Let us his shining footsteps trace,
>   Let us his steadfast faith pursue;
> Follow this follower of the Lamb,
> And conquer all through Jesus' name.'"

October 22*d*. Have just returned from a week's visit at the orphan home of my friend, sister T. It was a week to be remembered, for its holy communings and precious seasons of prayer, especially at our "sacred hour of ten." Spent some of the time in writing. We wrote, by request, the particulars of brother Law's death, for the *Guide*. While thus engaged, his presence seemed so near that I was forced to lay aside my pen, and give vent to the overpowering feelings of the soul in tears and praises to Him who is "the resurrection and the life," and who will bring with him those who "sleep in Jesus."

While there, learned of the death of Mr. C.,

a man of promise and influence, whom we had, with others, unitedly urged to an immediate surrender to Christ, on the Coldwater Campground. He faithfully promised that he would set about the work immediately; and said that we might know, when we thought of him (he was then about to leave the ground), that he was living a Christian life; that all earthly considerations should not hinder in the immediate work of saving the soul; and, to make this promise still stronger and more sacred, if possible, wrote his name in my Hymn-book, under the hymn:

> "Lord, in the strength of grace,
> With a glad heart and free,
> Myself, my residue of days,
> I consecrate to thee.
>
> Thy ransom'd servant, I
> Restore to thee thine own;
> And from this moment, live or die,
> To serve my God alone."

Thus we parted. But O, the broken vow! How it will rise up in the Day of Judgment, to his condemnation!

Instead of yielding to the just, acknowledged claims of God, he plunged more fully into the world than ever before, little realizing that,

> "Soon, borne on time's most rapid wing,
> Should death command him to the grave,

> Before God's bar his spirit bring,
> And none be found to hear or save."

In three short months from the making of that pledge, upon a bed of death he said to those around him: "The remembrance of the unkept promise made to those sisters at C., has been with me by night and day—a thorn in my pillow, a barbed arrow in my heart; and the thought of that broken vow is now filling my heart with anguish; and if I live I will immediately set about the work, but it is of no use now!" And thus he passed away to the spirit-land. How true that, "Whatsoever a man soweth, that shall he also reap!"

October 26th. "In all thy ways acknowledge Him, and he shall direct thy paths," is much on my mind.

> "Leave to his sovereign sway,
> To choose and to command."

December 1st. On the thirteenth of last month, was united in marriage to Rev. J. E. M'Allister, of the Michigan Conference. This step has not been taken without realizing the sacred obligations incurred, and the toils and sacrifices to be shared with the itinerant. But so emphatically do I feel it to be of the Lord, that, notwithstanding all my unworthiness and unfitness for a work so important, I should hardly dare (did my heart prompt) to refuse to say, "Whither thou goest, I will go; thy people shall be my people, and thy God my God."

We arrived at the parsonage at Leroy, Mr. M'Allister's field of labor, late in the afternoon of the fourteenth of last month, where we found a large company met to welcome us, with a hearty welcome, judging from the table groaning beneath its load of varieties.

Every thing was done that could be to make our coming among this people pleasant; and, had it not been for the suffering state of Mr. M'Allister, we could have asked no more. But our Father, who is too wise to err and too good to be unkind, ordered that the cup of happiness should for the time be exchanged for one of sorrow. His disease (hemorrhage of the stomach) increased with rapidity until the eighteenth, when word came that his physician had said he could "do no more for him; there was no hope of life."

With feelings indescribable, after writing telegrams to absent friends, we retired, to be "alone with God;" feeling that new strength must be imparted, or we should sink beneath the sudden, unlooked-for sorrow upon us.

We thought of the past: how hopes fondly

cherished, by one dark wave of sorrow were forever crushed, and laid in broken fragments at our feet; and of the grace that, amid it all, had sustained, enabling us, in joyous anticipation, to look forward to the time when these broken fragments, clothed with immortal beauty, would be all gathered again by Him who hath declared, "The very hairs of your head are all numbered;" and, with earnest pleadings, we beseeched the Throne for *present* grace, to enable us now, while in a land of strangers, to magnify that grace which saves to the uttermost; and arose to our feet with our feelings best expressed in the language of the prophet, "The work of righteousness shall be peace: and the effect of righteousness, quietness and assurance forever."

As we re-entered Mr. M'Allister's sick-room, we said to a dear brother in Christ present, "We must have a season of prayer." And at his bedside we bowed, while brother Sprague talked with God as friend with friend; pleading, if it might be God's will, for the restoration of the health of their pastor; and, in broken utterances, we followed. O, there were, at that hour, turnings away from human instrumentalities to the "balm in Gilead," to the "Great Physician" there; and prayer entered the ear of the Most High. Heaven and earth blended into one! Glory crowned the mercy-seat, while together my husband and myself shouted aloud the praises of our adorable Redeemer!

From that hour, there was a marked change. His physician, coming in soon after, said, "You are better." His disease abated, and he is now about, though unable as yet to do effective work on his circuit; but is steadily improving, and says that he must forever acknowledge that he owes his recovery to the *direct* answer to the prayers of those who on that Sabbath kneeled at his bedside. Our soul responds, "To God alone be glory!"

> "Thus to the Lord I raised my cry;
> He heard me from his holy hill;
> At his command the waves rolled by:
> He beckoned, and the winds were still."

February 12, 1867. Mr. M'Allister has just closed a series of meetings here, in which some twenty-five have been converted.

God has been with his people in power, hearing and answering prayer. Some very interesting young people, in whose salvation we became very much interested, give clear evidence of a change of heart and promise of usefulness.

Several evenings of this meeting were marked with more than ordinary interest.

One Sabbath evening, as Mr. M'Allister was

about to close the public services, suddenly he was overcome with burden of soul for the unconverted present; and fell upon his knees and commenced pleading aloud for their salvation, that the insulted Spirit that, day after day, had of late been so deeply moving their hearts, might not take its everlasting flight. This same burden at the same moment fell upon several others present, and, for over an hour, the earnest prayers of these were heard, while the unconverted looked on with amazement, obliged to confess, "Lo, God is here!" and quite a number arose, asking for prayer in their behalf.

One young man, who was specially remembered, and who afterward yielded to his pungent conviction, remarked that, during that hour, he had so clear a sense of the awful presence of God and of his own unsaved condition that it would have hardly been possible for him to rise from his seat.

Another evening, while Mr. M. was yet preaching, a young man arose from his seat in the back part of the house, starting, as we supposed, for the door, but reeling like a drunken man as he went, supporting himself as best he could through the aisle, until he reached the chair where Mr. M. was standing, in front of the desk, when he fell upon his knees, exclaiming: "PRAY FOR ME!"

and, before he arose to his feet, was happily converted to God. He is a young man of promise, and bids fair, if faithful, for a future of much usefulness.

May we be permitted to meet these when we shout our harvest-home!

February 25th. We are much drawn out in prayer for S. E. Leroy. God's people there are very few and feeble, and so many following the "Lo, here!" and "Lo, there!" of the world. Can human instrumentality reach these, hardened by the deceitfulness of sin? We turn away from trust in human help, to Him who hath said: "ASK OF ME, and I shall give thee" even "the heathen for thine inheritance, and the uttermost parts of the earth for thy possession."

March 24th. During the past few weeks, have been permitted to labor incessantly in the vineyard of the Lord; and our hearts have been gladdened by witnessing a gracious outpouring of his Spirit at S. E. Leroy. Some forty or fifty have turned their feet from the ways of sin and folly into paths of pleasantness and peace. Husbands and wives, young men and maidens, together came, seeking the "pearl of great price;" and even the gray-headed sought not in vain.

Thank God for the privilege of directing these burdened, sin-sick souls to the Lamb for sinners slain, and of rejoicing with them when newly clothed in the robes of praise; and though during these weeks I was the only female present to labor at the altar, I would here record, to the glory of God's grace, that I was wonderfully helped, proving, O so sweetly, "My grace is sufficient!" O, the preciousness of the privilege of being permitted to stand up amid the hosts of sin, raising the blood-stained banner of the cross! I ask no higher honor; I seek no greater happiness.

"Might I enjoy the meanest place
Within Thy house, O God of grace;
Not tents of ease, or thrones of power,
Should tempt my feet to leave thy door."

That God is not slack concerning his promises, as some men count slackness, we know; and, as year after year is revealing to us more and more of the mystery of godliness, again and again, in plainer and yet plainer characters, do we set to our seal, "God is true;" but at this meeting we learned new lessons of

THE POWER OF FAITH.

STREAMS of living water were all around us, gushing forth; and the wilderness and solitary place of sin was "blossoming as the rose;" but

Satan's kingdom, which has so long had dominion, is in danger, and infidels and spiritualists must needs come to the rescue. Who shall triumph? Shall the few followers of the lowly Nazarene expect to be victors when the contest is so unequal? But we hear the command of our Captain, "Go FORWARD!" and, knowing in whom we trust, we obey. Evening service arrives, and a crowded house, with but a few to stand up for Christ, betokens the need of special help. One sat in the congregation whose faith was in unison with the faith of him who had it in charge, who had learned the worth of prayer; and, as that embassador of Christ arose to plead with sinners to be reconciled to God, these words to that one were presented, "This is the confidence that we have in Him, that if we ask any thing according to his will he heareth us; and if we know that he hear us, whatsoever we ask, we know that we have the petition that we desired of him;" and with it the inquiry, "Have you the faith to ask for present victory over these opposing persons, and a new impetus to this work?" For a moment faith wavered. The tempter reasoned, "Circumstances are against it: the crowded house, the presence of those who so earnestly oppose the work;" while the Spirit whispered, "But it is in accordance with the will of God that salvation come to this house to-night; that the Word be so clothed with power from on high that *present* fruit be the result; and the power is yours, of every disciple of Christ, to claim it."

Not daring the non-exercise of this power of faith, we stepped out, upon the promise. From that moment, access seemed given into the audience-chamber of the Unseen, and steadily we held our petition, presented in the name of Jesus, before the throne, awaiting results; saying to the flesh, which cried, "It can not be," "Keep silence before the Lord;" until the answer came, in the burning words of truth that fell from the sacred desk; in the commanding manner of him who spoke in honor of his Divine Master, "who spake as never man spake;" and in the rush that was made by many, at its close, for the altar of prayer.

One gray-headed man, who sat near the center of the congregation, who, but a few evenings previous, had, in anger, left before service closed, arose, and, facing his former friends—the enemies of the cross of Christ—in a manner which thrilled the audience, said, "The Spirit and the Bride say, Come! and I am going; come with me!" and then hastened to the altar, followed by nine, men of influence, mostly heads of families; and we bow with them, presenting their case to the Father, knowing that our God heareth prayer.

For a few days the work moves steadily on: then, again, we behold the enemies of the cross in battle array. A text is given, from which the minister of Christ consents to speak, and pains is taken to have one, previously not an attendant of the meeting, present; one in whom those earnest workers for their master, "the great arch-deceiver," have confidence as a leader and helper. He spends the evening taking notes, while the two-edged sword—the eternal word of truth, given by themselves—is wielded against them. Again we flee to our Rock of Defense, presenting the Word which abideth forever, and again claim its fulfillment. The result is, he in whom they had expected so strong a re-enforcement remains to pray. And night after night finds him with the people of God, contending for the truths of our holy Christianity. And again, as we look upon him, are we led to exclaim: "Now thanks be unto God, which always causeth us to triumph in Christ!"

Again, it is Sabbath evening. We are met, with a few of the disciples of Christ, for social prayer. Worn and weary in body and mind, the adversary seems ready to withstand every onward step. We opened our mouth in prayer; but power seemed lacking, power to prevail with God; and, with a feeling of unrest of soul, we arose to our seat. We were earnest in the desire to make all these means of grace steps in the way to lead us nearer God and heaven, and therefore were led to ask of the Lord to cause even the experience of this evening to result in his glory; and, asking calmly and confidingly an increase of the power of a life of faith in the soul, arose to testify for Christ, expressing present experience, and our present petition and expectation of its fulfillment.

The coming week was one of unusual spiritual conflict, causing the exclamation, "Why go I mourning because of the oppression of the enemy?" the adversary oft suggesting the inquiry, "Where now is the answer to your petition?"

Sabbath morning came, and we repaired to the house of God. During the opening prayer, while not drawn out in any unusual manner, our soul was suddenly filled to overflowing. The baptism of the Holy Spirit is upon us, and we are constrained to give vent to the fountain within in expressions of praise and flowing tears. Wondering at such condescension, why we are fed so bountifully, we look up inquiringly to the Giver—and quick the response, "This is the answer to your petition of last Sabbath evening."

Thus, as we onward urge our way, are we permitted to realize the answer to the prayer of faith, in "new creations" in our own and the souls of others.

> "This is the victory:
> Before our faith they fall;
> Jesus hath died for you and me—
> Believe, and conquer all."

CHAPTER VIII.

April 23d.

REV. J. JENNINGS.

"Lift not thou the wailing voice,
　　Weep not; 't is a Christian dieth!
Up where blessed saints rejoice,
　　Ransomed now, the spirit flyeth.
High in Heaven's own light he dwelleth;
Full the song of triumph swelleth;
Freed from earth and earthly failing,
Lift for him no voice of wailing."

HAVE just learned of the death of Rev. J. Jennings, of the Michigan Conference. He was long a great sufferer; but we can not look back upon that noble life—given a blessing to those among whom he has ministered in holy things—and the peaceful, triumphant exit to the land of the "living," without exclaiming, "Let me live the life, and die the death, of the righteous!"

He had hearkened diligently to the commands

of God, and his peace was "as a river," deepening and widening until it emptied its mighty, unruffled waters into eternity.

When told by his counsel of physicians, for the first, that his disease was cancer of the stomach, and that he must soon die, the physician who held his hand, with his finger upon his pulse, remarked, that there was not the least flutter, not a beat quicker. Ah, heaven's gate to him stood ajar! Glory was gilding the pathway there, lighting up the valley, and he feared not to enter.

Though constitutionally not emotional, peace—deep, abiding peace—best expressing the state of mind in which he lived, while Rev. R. C. Crawford, who, but a few days before his death, visited him, at his request was singing at his bedside,

> "Come all ye saints to Pisgah's mountain ;
> Come view your home beyond the tide ; . . .
>
> O, the prospect it is so transporting,
> And no danger I fear from the tide !
> Let me go to the home of the Christian—
> Let me stand robed in white by his side ;"

he became very exultant, and at its close, exclaimed, "O, won't I jump and leap and shout when safe landed on the other shore!"

We could but wonder, as we visited his sickroom, which always seemed privileged for its nearness to heaven, why upon him, in the prime of life, beloved by all, eminent for usefulness as a minister of the Gospel, death should be permitted to fix his seal. Reason argued, so much needed! Brethren in toil, cultivators together of Immanuel's land, gather around, and would fain detain the spirit bursting its bonds, for he is a leader in the van of the host. But our vain questioning was silenced.

A short respite from pain is given, and the sufferer sleeps. A heavenly smile plays upon the countenance; light from the upper world is reflected upon that face of clay. The eyes gently open, and are directed toward the darkened window. The lips move, and we catch the whisper, "O, how beautiful! how beautiful!" His weeping companion approaches, saying, "Yes, it is a lovely day; shall I throw open the shutter so that you may once again look upon the beauties of nature?" The countenance, already radiant with heaven's own light, beams with more than angelic glory as he responds, "O, I see beyond the shutters—far beyond the shutters!"

Reason is hushed. Faith speaks, "Our light affliction, which is but for a moment, worketh for us a far more exceeding and eternal weight of glory." "Clouds and darkness are round about him; righteousness and judgment are the habitation of his throne." How beautiful, how full of meaning to us, was that lesson!

Are the storms of earth howling around our habitation, threatening to ingulf amid the waves upon which we are tossed? Are the habiliments of mourning ours? Has affliction thrown her sable garb over all nature? A wanderer, darkness over us, our pillow a stone? Are we in poverty's vale? Has disease laid its wasting hand upon us? Faith looks beyond the darkened window, pierces through the gloom of the things seen, and takes us beyond, to the things unseen, "beyond the shutters!" There all is light.

We hear the voice. Its joyful echo comes penetrating the darkest gloom of earthly sorrow: "Behold, I have loved thee with an everlasting love." "He that overcometh shall inherit all things," whether he be from a throne of earthly glory, or a weeping Lazarus from the rich man's gate. If we walk amid earth's pollutions with garments white, we shall "have right to the tree of life, and enter through the gate into the city."

> "There, no bond is ever sever'd;
> Partings, claspings, sob and moan,
> Midnight waking, twilight weeping,
> Heavy noontide,—all are done."

July 1st. During last month was permitted to attend the camp-meeting on Coldwater District. Here we were permitted to renew the precious acquaintances of the past; also, to meet again our beloved friends, Doctor and Mrs. Palmer. It was sweet to commune together on earth; to tell each other of the dealings of God with our souls in the past; to labor together for the salvation of others. But there cometh a happier, more glorious meeting! *Here*, when we meet, tears will fall as we look upon the vacant places of those who have forever ceased their labors upon earth. We list in vain for their words of comfort, of holy triumph, in the feasts of love. *There*, there will be no vacant place, no voice missing, while the redeemed millions join in the new song "unto Him that loved us, and washed us from our sins in his own blood!"

> "Blest hour, when righteous souls shall meet,
> Shall meet to part no more;
> And with celestial welcome greet
> On an immortal shore!"

This meeting was greatly blessed to my own establishment in the way of faith; and my companion and myself were greatly encouraged to go forth, endeavoring, as we go, to scatter Scriptural holiness, contending earnestly for the faith delivered to the saints.

Sabbath evening, the last that some of us were permitted to remain on the ground, will ever be remembered. Expecting to part in the morning, and most likely never all meet again until the morning of the resurrection, after the public services, a few of us gathered in our beloved presiding elder's tent to reconsecrate ourselves to our lifework; and, while pleading the "promise of the Father" to requalify us for our mission, the baptism of the Holy Ghost came upon us. The form of the "Fourth" appeared in our midst, and in awe we exclaimed: "How dreadful is this place! This is none other but the house of God, and this is the gate of heaven."

My bodily powers, as were others, were prostrated. My lips could not have uttered a sentence; but it was

> "The speechless awe that dares not move,
> And all the silent heaven of love."

If this be seeing through a glass darkly, what will it be when we see face to face? *That* may be our next meeting with the loved ones with whom we that night so sweetly communed in foretaste of the better, when this mortal shall have put on immortality. Until then, may Christ's righteousness be our beauty, our daily dress! for, as Dr. Palmer remarked, "Our Father is rich enough to provide all his children with white raiment for every day."

O Father, save me from garments having spot or wrinkle or any such thing!

> "Finish then thy new creation;
> Pure and spotless let us be;
> Let us see thy great salvation
> Perfectly restored to thee."

From here we went to our Albion feast of tabernacles. Here God met his people in his own leafy temple, and "his candlestick was gold." O, what infinite condescension of the Holy One that inhabiteth eternity! "And I will pray the Father: and he shall give you another Comforter, that he may abide with you forever." Glory to his name! Humanity still walks and talks with Jesus.

On Sabbath of this meeting, a number banded together to pray especially for the descent of the Holy Spirit upon the multitude upon the ground, and every interval between public services found these together in a tent, pleading the promise, "If ye abide in me and my words abide in you, ye shall ask what ye will, and it shall be done unto you," for this one thing. Some looked on in somewhat of amazement that a few of Christ's disciples should expect to hold in check that vast multitude by the simple prayer of faith. Evening service came, and oft we heard the exclamation, as we looked upon the large, attentive, and perfectly orderly congregation, "I never saw it in this wise! What does this mean?" while these few importunate ones, strong in faith, gave glory to God.

There *is* a God in Israel that heareth prayer. O, when shall the Church of the living God realize her privilege in this respect? The power is already given the army of the Captain of our salvation, would she but use it, to take the world. He, to-day, is speaking to the Christian Church, in words not to be misunderstood," "Hitherto have ye asked nothing in my name: ask, and ye shall receive, that your joy may be full."

> "O, wondrous power of faithful prayer!
> What tongue can tell the Almighty grace!
> God's hands or bound or open are,
> As Moses or Elijah prays."

August 18*th*. Since my last date, have seemingly been brought very near death's door, by heart-disease and partial paralysis. Some of the time it seemed but a step over to the other shore. Felt to say:

> "Hark! they whisper: angels say,
> Sister spirit, come away!"

Yet I had a strong desire, if it were the will of the All-wise Father, to live; not but what all looked bright and joyful! O no! It was all light about the river: could hardly see even the shadow of the conquered monster, Death; but, as I looked over the past of my life, so little had been done for the cause of Christ, so few stars gathered for the diadem of the Redeemer, and so many thronging the broad road that I would fain bring home to God and heaven, that I could but feel that, if Infinite Wisdom saw fit, it were preferable to live, even though it be to go forth *weeping*, bearing precious seed, that I might finally come again "with rejoicing," bringing my sheaves with me. And then there were loved ones, who need I should stay. God has heard their prayer.

"Still let me live, Thy blood to show,
Which purges every stain."

September 4th. Have just been permitted to attend a camp-meeting on our own circuit. It was appointed amid many discouragements; but we heard the command, "Go forward;" "Lo, I am with you alway;" and, looking away from human encouragement, the meeting was appointed, and we betook us to the place of prayer, asking of Him who heareth prayer to incline the hearts of his people to leave their worldly cares, and go and sacrifice unto the Lord.

This prayer was answered beyond our expectations, and eternity alone will tell the results of the meeting. Many of our own members, as well as those on adjoining charges, were here enabled to realize their calling's glorious hope— "inward holiness;" and others were taken out of the "horrible pit, out of the miry clay," and their feet placed upon "the Rock," and a "new song" put in their mouths, even praise unto our God. To God alone be all the glory!

During this meeting my companion, who had it in charge, was wonderfully helped in his arduous duties; and, beyond the expectation of my friends, though very feeble in body, I was permitted to mingle in the assembly of God's saints. And there we again set to our seal, "God is true." With newly-learned notes of praise, we there raised our "Ebenezer," having come hither on our pilgrimage home, by the help of God still looking forward to the finding of happier ground than ever we have found while in the tented grove.

September 20th. Have just returned from our Annual Conference, held at Lansing. Went asking that that mingling with God's chosen might be made a special blessing to my own and the souls of others; and I here record it as one of the best weeks of my life.

Our social prayer and converse circles at

brother Johnson's—the dear family with whom we boarded—were made a lasting blessing. Several of those occupying positions of usefulness, there sought and found the rest of faith; and went to their newly appointed fields of labor with renewed courage and increased strength to labor in the vineyard of the Lord.

Our Sabbath morning Conference love-feast was a season of unusual interest. Most of those who spoke gave a clear testimony of the present witness of the Spirit to the efficacy of the blood of the atonement to cleanse from all sin. God be praised that this "central idea" of our holy Christianity is gaining ground in our state! The sons of Levi are being purified. The watchmen ARE giving the certain sound.

In answer to the united prayer of God's people, Zion is arising, is putting on her strength.

The morning does of hope and joy foretell: the light is dawning; the morning breaketh!

The prayer Christ himself taught us, "Thy kingdom come; thy WILL be done in earth, as it is in heaven," will be answered.

We are returned to Leroy. Have commenced the year with renewed consecrations of all to Christ. Never felt more the worth of immortal souls than at present.

December 20th.

> "Joy for thee, happy friend! thy bark hath passed
>   The rough sea's foam!
> Now the long yearnings of thy soul are stilled:
> Home; home! thy peace is won, thy heart is filled,
>   Thou art gone home!"

To loved ones in Christ, with whom so often in the past we have sat in "heavenly places" in Christ, the cry has been made, "Behold, the Bridegroom cometh: go ye out to meet him!" But long had they been watching, clad in bridal attire, with lamps trimmed and brightly burning.

> "*Now* their lamps are gleaming from the distant shore,
> Where no billows threaten, where no tempests roar."

MRS. HARRIET BROCKWAY.*

They who, without a murmur, have given their loved ones to the grave, and with tearless eye—looking upon the heaven-side of the dark cloud gathered about their pathway—have said, "The Lord gave and the Lord hath taken away: blessed be the name of the Lord!" know something of the victories of the cross. But the mother who, with the question pressing hard upon her, "Who will shield my daughters? who will guide my boys?" has placed the hands of the little group into the hand of God, and then,

* Wife of Rev. N. L. Brockway, Michigan Conference.

with a smile, has turned aside into the valley, knows more. *This* victory was sister Brockway's.

While in the midst of the swelling tide, in triumph she exclaimed, "Strong consolation! strong consolation! who have fled to Christ for refuge!"

By her words, we were reminded of a beautiful illustration we recently heard Bishop Clark use, while preaching from "The word of the Lord is tried:"

"A lady came to the bank of a swollen river, whose waters were foaming and dashing wildly upon the rocks beneath, which could only be crossed by a single foot-plank.

"She placed her feet upon the plank, took a step or two, when, affrighted by the angry roar below, she retraced her steps, and again stood upon the shore. Then, again summoning new courage, her feet were placed upon the single foot-piece; but her head grew dizzy as she saw, beneath, the splashing tide, and again in haste she retraced her steps, and stood upon the bank of the river. For a few moments she stood undecided, while with earnest desire she looked over the tide; then, with her eye fixed *upward*, with firm, steady step, she placed again her foot upon the plank, and, without faltering, reached in safety the desired shore.

"A friend who, from the opposite bank, had watched her, inquired, 'How dare you cross on that single plank, with those deep, angry waters foaming beneath?' She replied, 'Others, looking upward, had crossed over in safety; the plank had been tried; and, then, here were loved ones waiting for me!'"

O death! thy stream is bridged forever! Not all the combined forces of earth and hell can bear away the foundation thereof. A thousand Niagara's blended into one have here no power. "That by two immutable things, in which it was impossible for God to lie, we might have a strong consolation who have fled for refuge, to lay hold upon the hope set before us, which hope we have as an anchor of the soul, both sure and steadfast, and which entereth into that within the veil." "The Word of the Lord is tried;" our friends cross over the river in safety.

Sister Brockway was an earnest laborer in her Master's vineyard; and many, at the different places where, with her devoted companion, she has toiled, will "rise up and call her blessed."

We last met her on the Coldwater Campground, where she mingled with God's people, a joyful witness of the power of grace to save from sin. As she lived, so she died; and now is mingling with the host that have crossed the flood.

"Write, Blessed are the dead which die in the Lord, from henceforth; yea, saith the Spirit, that they may rest from their labors: and their works do follow them."

MRS. ELEUTHERIA CRANE.*

For forty-one years sister Crane shared with her devoted companion—who was prominent among the noble men who laid the foundation of the Church in our West—the toils and triumphs of the itinerant life. Many of her gathered sheaves have passed over before her; others will come after. She possessed in no usual degree the mind of Christ; and this, like the natural outgushing of a pure fountain, was constantly venting itself in acts of unselfishness. Of her we find written by a friend, who knew her well, the following:

"Modest and unobtrusive, she was still indefatigable. At the bedside of the sick and dying, in homes bereaved, and in the abodes of want, she was a ministering angel. In every place she lived, her name 'is as ointment poured forth.' Her piety was unpretending, but pervaded her whole life. She exhibited the spirit of Jesus. Repeatedly it is said: 'We never saw any thing

---

* Wife of Rev. Elijah Crane, Michigan Conference.

in her spirit or conduct we would have otherwise.' God's Word was her constant study and guide, God's house and ordinances her chief delight. Even in advanced age she was seldom absent from the public or social assembly. To the close of life she was a teacher in the Sabbath-school, and her class were tearful mourners at her grave.

"In the privacy of her own home her beautiful character shone with its sweetest luster. 'Her husband's heart trusted in her, and her children rise up and call her blessed.' It was a priceless privilege to dwell in a home pervaded by a presence so pure, so exalted; to be loved and guided by one so good and wise. The hospitalities of her home, the genial welcome, the unwearying tenderness, and the thoughtful care, will never be forgotten by hundreds.

"She sickened and died within one week; and thus was gratified an often-expressed desire that she might 'cease at once to work and live.' To the Church of her love, and to her sorrowing husband and children, she leaves the priceless legacy of her beautiful character and life, and the blessed assurance that 'they who sleep in Jesus will God bring with him.'"

"Servant of God, well done!
Thy glorious warfare's past;
The battle's fought, the race is won,
And thou art crowned at last."

By these bereavements, two itinerant homes have been made sad, O so sad and lonely! Two pillars of the Church have been removed. But they live in Zion above. There, " not one of the stakes thereof shall ever be removed, neither shall any of the cords thereof be broken."

December 28th. A Christmas-gift of "Life and Letters of L. L. Hamline." Read a few pages, and laid the book down with breathings of soul after God, and intense longings to know more of the inner life, the life of faith. O, how full of poverty this soul! How poor the offering it gives compared with such! Thou God of Jacob, of Elijah, breathe into my soul their faith, and then, O " Son of man!" stand confessed in all thy saving power! Am taking these aspirations of soul to the Father, pleading the merits of the Son. Am so unsatisfied with self, even with every effort to glorify God. O Father! art thou in this way already answering these soul-aspirations, and leading me nearer thyself?—causing me to see my poverty, that of thee I may buy "gold tried in the fire," that I may be rich; my blindness, that of thee I may have " eye-salve " wherewith to anoint mine eyes, that I may see? causing me to behold my nakedness, that of thee I may be provided with " white raiment?" Then

I thank thee for even my poverty of spirit; thank thee for humbling me in the dust, if need be. Only from this let me arise to glorify thee. Only let me, out of all my griefs, a bethel raise, and be brought nearer thee, and I'm content.

January 12, 1868. Sweet is the day of sacred rest. Deprived of the blessings of the sanctuary by ill health; but in my surrendered heart there is consecrated a house of prayer.

Thousands, while I write, are mingling in the assembly of God's saints. Were I permitted to be among them, my glad heart might learn new themes, new songs of praise. My soul seems in communion with the pure in heart, both here and on the other side of the narrow stream which divides the Church; with the loved ones in Christ, east, west, north, and south, in whose company I have taken so much delight, and the multitude whom I have never met, but whose acquaintance I shall form in heaven. Have thought of the ecstasy of joy I should know were a company of these gathered upon earth, and I permitted to sit among them, and listen to the words that would fall from their lips as they told of the victories of the cross; then, in blissful anticipation, my mind reaches forward to that, not day, but eternity, I shall be permitted to spend with these, and *more!*

> "That great mysterious Deity,
> We soon with open face shall see;
>   The beatific sight
> Shall fill the heavenly courts with praise,
> And wide diffuse the golden blaze
>   Of everlasting light."

O, wondrous thought, that I, even I, shall be thus exalted!—raised from my low estate, and made a king and priest unto God! O, wondrous exchange! my garment of guilt, pollution, shame, and sorrow, exchanged for one of spotless purity, and thus be made meet for an inheritance with the saints in light! What a mystery, yet what a glorious truth, that faith in a crucified, risen Redeemer, should produce a change so great! Not strange that angels should wonder at the love that crowns us!

CHAPTER IX.

May 1st.

REV. ELIJAH CRANE.*

"And if the brightest diadem,
  Whose gems of glory purely burn
    Around the ransomed ones in bliss,
Be evermore reserved for them,
Who here, through toil and sorrow, turn
    Many to righteousness ;
May we not think of thee as wearing
That star-like crown of light, and bearing,
Amid heaven's white and blissful band,
The fadeless palm-branch in thy hand ;
And joining, with a seraph's tongue,
In that new song the elders sung?"

THE pillars of Zion below are fast being removed to Zion above. O, that the mantles of those who have so long blessed the Church and the world with their example and labors, as *they* vanish from sight, may fall upon those who take their place!

* Michigan Conference.

Inadequate are we to the work of penning the tribute our heart would dictate to the memory of this champion of Jesus. Memories of the past, personal words of comfort and strength given, rush upon us; and, with those who mourn him as father, we would weep.

Those clear pointings from the sacred desk to the "blood that cleanseth;" the testimonies for years listened to, of the power of a life of faith; those prayers leading so near the Throne, causing one to forget all but the one thought: "We are in the presence of God,"—how the memory falls upon us as "ointment poured forth," and we can but exclaim, Though dead, he yet lives on earth as truly as in heaven!

For forty-seven years, immortal monuments have been marking the pathway of this devoted minister of Christ here; and a monument of immortal souls, saved through his instrumentality, is before the Throne. His "record is on high."

Little did we think, when upon our heart fell the saddening intelligence, "Sister Crane is no more," that so soon they would be reunited in the mansion made ready for their rest. No one visited him during his last hours but that felt to say, "If THIS be death, 't is happiness to die!"

To his daughter, Mrs. Daugherty, who—after a week's absence—being overcome with emotion upon coming into his room and seeing him so greatly changed, he said, "I am going very fast; but O, I wish you could see it as I see it!" She said, "How does it seem, pa?" He replied: "O, delightful! most delightful! I have naturally a strong love of life, and although I never, since becoming a Christian, have *feared death*, yet I have always felt an aversion to the grave; but now there is no spot of earth so attracts as a place beside your mother. I have felt, for weeks past, as though I were more a resident of the spirit-land than of this; am always surprised when I awake and find myself still an inhabitant of earth."

At another time, he asked of her, "Do you recollect what Bunyan says of the land of Beulah?" On receiving an affirmative reply, he said, "*I* KNOW ALL ABOUT *it now.*" To another daughter, during a severe paroxysm of pain, when all thought him near his departure, he said, "Ah, my daughter! the separation will be but short; to me it looks like no more than stepping into another room!"

The Sabbath before his death, at a communion-service in his room, he said, "How I wish I had strength to talk for a little while to these brethren and sisters in Christ, of the wonderful view I have had this morning of the atonement; of the wonderful manner in which the atonement, the glories of redemption, has opened up before me!"

Upon this occasion, he requested that nothing should be sung of dying, but spoke of the hymn with the words,

> "Sing of His dying love,
> Sing of his rising power,"

which was sung; during which the words, "Glory! glory!" seemed breathed as from a soul who had already joined in the sweeter song of "Moses and the Lamb" above.

Thus passed the closing hours of this servant of God. With him, at eventide, it was light, and around him has broken the eternal morn of heaven.

May 5*th*. Have been deprived, for some months past, on account of ill-health, from entering actively into labor for the salvation of souls. My present allotment seems to be suffering, instead of *doing* the will of God.

Missives from loved Christian friends came laden with tidings of battles and victories; news of sinners returning home; and, as I have perused these precious remembrances, oft have I found my heart silently exclaiming, "O, that I too might in some way, however humble, enter into personal, active effort for the salvation of others!" It has often seemed that a few hours, even, of such labor would be a precious boon.

Deprived in a great degree of accustomed communion with Christian friends, the mind affected by the weakness of the body, the adversary of late has seemed to take special delight in taunting suggestions of my want of the spirit of labor, my lack of zeal in the cause of my Master; and that this was sufficient to convince me that I had lost my abiding in Christ,—against which I had but one standard to raise up, "The just shall live by faith."

This morning, at our sacred hour of ten, I was led to ask that the Lord would give to my soul an earnest hungering and thirsting after righteousness, and that thus these accusations of Satan but be used for my advancement in the way of holiness.

Realized through the day an answer to this petition; and though my mind was much occupied in surrounding cares, in the midst of these often found my soul going out in aspiration for a fresh anointing, the anointing that abideth.

At evening family devotion, these breathings became so intense that I asked of the Lord some promise upon which anew to rest my faith. Immediately, with wonderful power, these words were applied: "And the very God of peace sanctify you wholly: and I pray God your whole spirit and soul and body be preserved blameless unto the coming of our Lord Jesus Christ. Faithful is he that calleth you who also will do it."

Preserved blameless! O, the depth of meaning in those two words! Can it be that mortal should be so transformed, so raised from his fallen state? Blameless in the searching gaze of a holy God? Blameless before the multitude before the throne, who delight to cry, "Holy, holy is the Lord of hosts?" O grace! it was thou contrived the way of so wondrous a salvation—grace, that laid the shining way from earth's pollutions to heaven's glories; grace, that taught my wandering feet to tread the narrow way; and, when forever saved in heaven, grace shall swell the song of a sinner saved by its power. 'T is enough; and, satisfied with all Thy dealings, whether joyous or afflictive, I rest me in thy will.

September 4th. At Conference, at Three Rivers. Was deeply impressed, this morning, by the remarks of Bishop Ames to the class of candidates to deacon's orders. His remarks upon the growth of the inner life were especially blessed to me. Among others, this sentence thrilled my soul: "In this onward march, no one owns the lot in front of you." O, how my soul goes out in strong desire to know more of this "knowledge in Christ Jesus!" Heights I see before me; depths there are yet unfathomed; lengths and breadths of this love of Christ, fellowship with the Father and Son, of which I know so little. Shall I be satisfied when, with the redeemed from every tongue, I stand upon Zion's heights? I shall know more when I see him as he is, the King in his beauty; but eternity will be none too long for the revealing of the mystery unknown.

March 19, 1869.

> "His slender sail
> Ne'er felt the gale;
> He did but float a little way,
> And putting to the shore,
> While yet 't was early day,
> Went calmly on his way,
> To dwell with us no more.
>
> He seemed a cherub who had lost his way,
> And wandered hither; so his stay
> With us was short, and 't was most meet
> That he should be no delver in earth's clod,
> Nor need to pause and cleanse his feet,
> To stand before his God—
> O, blest word—evermore!"

Have just returned from Litchfield, where we went on Wednesday. Almost the first words of greeting were, "Little Brucie's dead!" How sadly the intelligence fell upon our heart! Could it be that those active limbs were lifeless; that those little feet had forever ceased their pattering; that the music of that voice was forever hushed, and the itinerant home of our dear brother and sister Hoag so suddenly made desolate?

We remembered the text of Scripture quoted so beautifully wrong, in his childish forgetfulness: "Blessed are the pure in heart"—slowly repeated several times, in vain trying to get the latter clause, when, suddenly catching the beauty of the inspiration, he added, "for God is ever with them." And we thought, Ah! the lesson he is now learning as no earthly instructor could teach, the blessedness of "God ever with them;" for he is *forever with God.*

True, the light of an earthly dwelling has forever gone out, and a little mound, and a stone marking where his form lies, must soon, in the wanderings to and fro of the publisher of the news of a risen Redeemer, be left to the care of strangers; but there is a family gathering, a reunion coming—not in this vale of tears, where fears of parting always chill, but in the beautiful mansion above, beside the crystalline stream, where flowers, which he so dearly loved upon earth, bloom immortal. There little Brucie waits the father and mother and weeping sister, upon whom a great sorrow has early fallen.

We did not wonder at the exclamation of our dear sister Hoag on the morning after his funeral, as she looked upon his little boots, his cap, the little saw he used, and the toys scattered here and there: "It seems as though I could not remove these from our sight. They make it seem more as though he were coming back to us." And yet we felt to magnify the grace that enabled those stricken hearts calmly amid their tears to say, "The Lord gave, and the Lord hath taken away; blessed be the name of the Lord!" "He can not come to us, but we shall go to him."

During the visions of last night, after mingling our tears together at their family altar, where was missed the sweet voice lisping,

"Now I lay me down to sleep,"

I beheld sister Hoag standing as a teacher of a large Bible-class, having herself chosen for the lesson, "That the trial of your faith, being much more precious than that of gold which perisheth, though it be tried with fire, might be found unto praise and honor and glory at the appearing of Christ." After having very clearly discussed the manner in which, by suffering, the graces of the

Christian are brought to a state of perfection, how often our Heavenly Father, in answer to our prayer to be made more Christ-like, permits to come upon our heart some great sorrow, thus weaning from earth, and proving to us the depth of meaning in "Whom the Father loveth he chasteneth," with a holy joy thrilling her countenance, she gave this beautiful illustration:

"Some years ago, a few ladies, who were met in a certain place for the study of the Scriptures, were reading the words, 'For he is like a refiner's fire and like fullers' soap; and he shall sit as a refiner and purifier of silver: and he shall purify the sons of Levi, and purge them as gold and silver;' when one remarked, 'There is something remarkable in the expression, "He shall sit as a refiner and purifier of silver."' After some conversation, they agreed that, during the coming week, and before their next meeting, one of their number should visit a silversmith, and report what might be said upon the subject. She went, and, without telling the object of her errand, begged to know from him the process of refining silver, which he fully described. 'But, sir,' said she, 'do you *sit* while the work of refining is going on?' 'O yes, Madam,' he replied; 'I must sit with my eye steadily fixed on the surface; for if the time necessary for refining be exceeded in the slightest degree, the silver is sure to be injured.' At once she saw the beauty and comfort of the expression, 'He shall sit as a refiner and purifier of silver,' and turned to leave the shop, when the silversmith detained her by adding 'that he only knew when the process of purifying was complete by seeing *his own image* reflected in the silver.'"

Ah yes; dear, afflicted one! Thou art being tried in the furnace of affliction. "Many shall be purified, and made white, AND TRIED;" but, blessed assurance that, the Heavenly Refiner sits by. Not one trial more than is necessary will be permitted; and when, in the morning of the Resurrection, shall be made known the "whys and wherefores," among thy list of blessings this shall stand foremost, "That thy heart has bled."

> "Grace comes as oft clad in the dusky robe
> Of Desolation, as in white attire."

June 10th. Am daily becoming more deeply impressed with the truth that the hiding-place of the Christian's power is sympathy with Jesus.

If we would reflect the image of Christ, we need to be much with him; with him in prayer, in meditation, and with him in our daily walk and intercourse with the world.

The Comforter is given that he may abide

with us forever, not as a transient guest, but an abiding friend; and if we thus abide with Christ, and he with us, will we not—though almost unconsciously to ourselves it may be, yet so perceptible to those with whom we associate—be changed into the image of the heavenly?

Go, for instance, into a room filled with rich perfume. When we go from thence, we shall carry with us of its odor; remain long away, and it is lost. Go again, and again we go out carrying with us of its fragrance. Thus it is with our intercourse with Him who is styled the "Rose of Sharon," and the "Lily of the Valley." If much with him, we shall partake of the loveliness of his character, of the sweetness of his spirit; and the unseen power accompanying his words, causing the utterance, "Never man spake as this man," shall be ours, attracting to the cross of Christ. O, it is prayer, communion with the Unseen, above all else, that will qualify us for usefulness in life, and for the "abundant" entrance to the city above!

> "Heaven's gates are not so highly arched
> As princes' palaces: they that enter there
> Must go upon their knees."

Said one, a few days since, of a dear friend who dwells in the secret place of the Most High, "I can not go into her presence without being blessed."

This truth, that they who thus walk and talk with Jesus will exert a power for good wherever they move, causing unbelief, in all its forms, to hide its distorted face, is beautifully expressed in the sentiment of the fable :

> "One day
> A wanderer found a lump of clay
> So redolent of rich perfume,
> Its odor scented all his room.
> 'What art thou?' was his quick demand;
> 'Art thou some gum from Samarcand?
> Or spikenard, in a rude disguise,
> Or other costly merchandise?'
> 'Nay, I am but a LUMP OF CLAY.'
> 'Then, whence this wondrous sweetness, say?'
> 'Friend, if the secret I disclose,
> I have been dwelling with the rose.'
> Meet parable! And will not those
> Who love to dwell with Sharon's Rose,
> Distill sweet fragrance all around,
> Though poor and mean themselves be found?
> Blest Lord, abide with us, that we
> May catch these odors fresh from thee!"

July 1st. How oft called to weep with those who weep and to mourn with those who mourn, while fast are being gathered our treasures for the Savior's diadem! A memorial from Rev. Mr. A. Daugherty, informing us of the recent death of their little Willie (aged ten years), reads as follows :

" This dear little boy, around whom clustered the brightest hopes and warmest love, has thus, just in the budding of his young life, been transplanted to

> 'The everlasting gardens,
> Where angels walk, and seraphs are the wardens;
> Where every flower brought safe through death's dark portals,
> Becomes immortal.'

"Through his most painful illness, of four weeks' duration, his sufferings were borne with the most lamb-like patience and sweetness, his intellect remaining unclouded to the very last. When asked how he would feel about going to the bright land whose inhabitants never say, 'I am sick!' he always replied that he was not at all afraid to go to the Savior, but did not like to leave papa and mamma. A few hours before his death, he cheerfully said, 'I guess I 'm going, mamma,' kissing good-bye to each, and saying to his weeping sister and brother, 'Do n't cry, Hattie; do n't cry Charlie!' and, again assuring his parents that he was 'not a bit afraid,' he sweetly fell asleep. . . .

"Reunited to his older brother, Eddie, his grandparents, and the blessed Savior, of whom he always delighted to hear, we know he will await, in the world of light, the coming of those he left in darkness and tears, yet who 'sorrow not as those who have no hope.'"

May our dear brother and sister Daugherty

find in Christ that consolation they so love to recommend to others, and finally, may they be a reunited family in the land of purity, to which so many of their number have of late passed!

> "The dear departed that have passed away
> To the still house of death, leaving thine own;
> The gray-haired sire that died in blessing thee,
> Mother, Eddie, and Willie, they who gave
> Thy home the light and bloom of paradise;
> They shall be thine again, when thou shalt pass,
> At God's appointment, through the shadowy vale,
> To reach the sunlight of th' immortal hills."

July 20th. Years ago I learned to say, "I thank Thee for my creation." This morning I say it with a fervor unknown before. Thou, O Father, readst it, down in the depths of this soul, that from that depth, while holy joy thrills the being, "I thank thee for this being"—a being created for so noble, high, and holy a purpose: "To glorify God and enjoy him forever;" and that, with this being, thou hast given to all such power for usefulness—a power that, if wisely wielded, may affect for good the eternal destiny, not only of those now surrounding us, but of souls yet to be. It may be but the smallest bark on the ocean, but it leaves its track behind! Waves are created by it, which in turn create others, and thus its influence is exerted on, and on, until each drop of the mighty deep, for miles, is affected by it. Thus it is with the lightest wave of influence. Once set in motion, it extends and widens until it reaches yonder eternal shore!

Listened recently, to J. B. Gough. Said he, during his lecture, in speaking of one whose name is unknown to the world except in abiding fruits, who recently died, leaving his family dependent: "They shall never want for the comforts of life, nor those children for the means of education. And why? Because, when I was but a lad, with a word of advice, he kindly put his hand upon my shoulder! That act saved me from the vortex of sin to which I was hastening, and placed my feet in the path of virtue."

> "A nameless man, amid a crowd
>   That thronged the daily mart,
> Let fall a word of hope and love,
>   Unstudied, from the heart.
> A whisper on the tumult thrown,
>   A transitory breath,
> It raised a brother from the dust;
>   It saved a soul from death.
> O germ! O fount! O, word of love!
>   O thought, at random cast!
> Ye were but little at the first,
>   But mighty at the last!"

We scatter seeds with careless hand, never expecting to see them again; but in ages yet to come, their fruit will appear either in poisonous weeds that shall mar the land, or in fruit ready to be gathered for garners above. O, the blessedness, O the responsibility, of life! One mistake, one neglect, may wreck unnumbered immortal souls! One act, one word, may save immortals from immortal woe! Then

> "Talk not of talents; what hast thou to do?
> Thy duty, be thy portion five or two.
> Talk not of talents; is thy duty done?
> Thou hadst sufficient, were they ten or one!"

KEYSTONE OF THE ARCH.

IN a meeting, not long since, where testimony was being given for Jesus, and where the glory of the Lord shone among the saints, a beloved minister, newly baptized for the work, said: "I am going home to write Holiness upon the keystone of the arch. Then shall the inhabitants of the rock sing, and the dwellers in the vales catch the flying joy."

God be praised, *this joy*, through the blood that cleanseth, is ours! Years since, "Holiness upon the keystone of the arch" enraptured our vision. We were among the dwellers in the vale. Dark mountains of unbelief towered on either side. We had read, it is true, in the legacy of the Christian, of a land where "thy sun shall no more go down, neither shall thy moon withdraw itself, for the Lord shall be thine everlasting light, and the days of thy mourning shall be ended;" had heard the voice, "And an highway shall be there, and a way, and it shall be called, the way of holiness. And the ransomed of the Lord shall return, and come to Zion with songs and everlasting joy upon their heads; they shall obtain joy and gladness, and sorrow and sighing shall flee away." But as it was in the days of a Saul of Tarsus, a Cornelius, that God's order was to lead to himself through human instrumentalities, so in our experience; and not until from direct testimony we had heard, "We speak that we do know, and testify that we have seen;" "I know for myself and not another, that the blood cleanseth from all sin," were we enabled to enter the rest of faith, and testify of the land of Beulah as no longer in the distance. And what was true in our experience, we find to be true in the experience of the Church, with but occasional exceptions, that God's order is, "That his Word and his Spirit lead to himself through our fellows as instruments."

DEFINITE TESTIMONY

WE believe to be the want of the Church at the present day, and is just where thousands are withholding from themselves and others rich, spiritual blessings. "Give, and it shall be given unto you: good measure, pressed down and shaken together, and running over," has a deep, spiritual meaning. This world of sin and spiritual darkness needs light. Not lamps lighted, and then put under a bushel; but those that, amid infidelity and opposing influences, shall shine with an even, clear luster, giving light to all around. Not the light of testimony by mouth alone; but the added one of holy lives. Holiness and consistent lives, we believe, go hand in hand. They are inseparable.

Not long since, we attended a meeting where, in public controversy, by some it was maintained that direct testimony with regard to the doctrine of holiness was unnecessary, and where reference was made to "the sisters who talk so much of holiness." For a moment, a feeling of complacency crept over us, as we thought, "We certainly are not meant." But this feeling, under the searchings of the Spirit, was suddenly swept away, and, instead, a feeling of shame, that upon this blessed doctrine of the Bible we were so silent; and to bear this cross, to more fully than ever before identify ourselves in sympathy with this cause, we thus write.

There are times when our Heavenly Father permits us to see ONLY THE CROSS; leaves us for a little while on the bleak side of the mountain. We feel the scorn of the world, realize the ignominy of the cross, see naught but the toil and suffering; but, while whispering, "Thy will be done," suddenly the crown, with all its glory, shining as the "brightness of the firmament," and as the "stars forever and ever," and the monument of souls before the Throne, bursts upon our vision; and, more firmly than ever before, we clasp to our hearts the cross.

> "The way to bliss lies not on beds of down,
> And he that has no cross deserves no crown."

Thus from that meeting we came. We've clasped anew the cross; in humility we lift the banner, with the motto, "Holiness unto the Lord!" and earnest is the prayer:

> "My faith as gold refine,
> Each grace and virtue prove,
> That in my spotless life may shine
> The light of perfect love."

Beloved reader: the question is with us, "Who shall thus upon the 'keystone of the arch' place 'Holiness?'" Famishing thousands throng our churches. Wealth, position, and influence they lay upon her altars. The preaching demanded by the times falls upon the ear of these worshipers; but inly there is a cry of unrest. Unsatisfied, the multitude are crying out for the Living Bread. Earnest is the longing of the soul for the smiting of the Rock, from whence shall flow the healing stream.

Minister of the Gospel: anointed of the Lord, and called to this one work, that of crying, "Behold the Lamb!"—we speak with humility, with reverence for the holy work—we look to you to place first in prominence before us the banner given to us as a people. O, let the way, by your teachings in accordance with the Word, be made so plain that "the wayfaring men, though fools, shall not err therein!" By your testimony, both in our public and social means of grace, O feed our hungry souls!

God be praised that the sons of Levi are being purified, that we have not need to say, "The former days were better than these;" but of the Lord there are being called those who "feed Jacob his people, and Israel his inheritance;" and sounds of rejoicing are coming from rock and vale. O, that this joy may increase until, from east, west, north, and south, like the noise of many waters, there shall come up the shout of triumph, of a world saved by the power of grace.

Class-leaders: you bear a share of this great responsibility. Members there are in your class who are looking—long have they been looking—for some Joshua, who shall from knowledge tell of the land flowing with milk and honey. O, lead on these weary ones into the land of rest from inbred sin!

Seeker of this joy—the spotless robe, the beauty of saints: enter by faith into the possession of thy purchased inheritance. No longer go mourning because of the oppression of the enemy. End the controversy between thy soul and God, causing thee so much of sorrow, and, by one act of entire consecration, lay thyself upon the altar that sanctifyeth the gift. Long have you been proving, by fastings, groans, and tears, it may be, that

> "No outward forms can make us clean;
> The leprosy lies deep within."

O, venture by faith, just as you are, upon the atoning merits of the world's Redeemer; and then from the Rock, saved entire, joyful shall be the song:

> "Jesus, thy blood, thy blood alone,
> Hath power sufficient to atone!
> Thy blood can make us white as snow;
> No Jewish types could cleanse us so."

Dear reader: hast thou found thy way into the temple, and still are at ease in Zion? Think not to shun your share in this work. Say not, as the wants of the Church, her lack of moral power, comes up before you, "Am I my brother's keeper?" Thou art. Around you, turn which way you will, are those who have a right, from your long experience it may be, or from your relation to or position in the Church, to look to you for spiritual food. Too few are the fathers, too few the mothers, in Israel. "For when for the time ye ought to be teachers, ye have need that some one teach you again which be the first principles of God; and are become such as have need of milk, and not of strong meat." Long has the baptism of power been awaiting you, and still what language so applicable as,—

> "Oft did I with the assembly join,
> And near Thy altar drew;
> A form of godliness was mine,
> The power I never knew?"

While thousands, it may be, looking to you as a leader in Zion, are, with you and through your influence, feeding upon husks, powerless for good. O arise! Shake thyself from the dust covering thy garments, wash by faith in the cleansing fountain, and put on thy beautiful array, "holiness," which is power. *Then* shall the "inhabitants of the rock sing," and the dwellers in the vale shall "catch the flying joy."

CHAPTER X.

OCTOBER 8TH. We are now settled at Moscow, our new home, for the year. Found, upon our arrival here, a large company met at the parsonage to welcome us, which greatly cheered our hearts.

How true, that the itinerant must be always ready to confess himself a stranger and pilgrim on the earth!

Two weary weeks have been spent in repairing, papering, and painting; and now we are looking with longing toward the already whitened harvest. Very few, we fear, are the reapers. O, so few to raise the standard of the cross!

This morning, while pleading before God for help, these words were strongly applied to my mind: "For ye shall go out with joy, and be led forth with peace: the mountains and the hills shall break forth before you into singing, and all the trees of the field shall clap their hands.

Instead of the thorn shall come up the fir-tree, and instead of the briar shall come up the myrtle-tree: and it shall be to the Lord for a name, for an everlasting sign that shall not be cut off."

February 20, 1869. Several weeks have passed in most earnest extra work for the prosperity of Zion, and the salvation of souls. A few have sought and found pardon, and the Church has taken higher ground in experience; but opposing influences are strong. Infidelity has long had the ground, and fearful is the contest. But, God be praised, we know that, sooner or later, *Truth shall triumph!*

Have been strengthened in reading of the rivers Arve and Rhone, whose waters meet but do not mingle—"the one, with its waters of heavenly blue, which it is almost worth a pilgrimage to see; the other, dark and muddy, because of the clayey soil through which it runs, and the glaciers by which it is surrounded. For miles they run with no barrier between, except their own innate repulsion; and for a long time the struggle is doubtful. But if we follow them far down into the valley, we find that the Rhone has conquered, and filled the whole surface of the valley with its own emblematic blue." "As I live, saith the Lord, all the earth shall be filled with the glory of the Lord."

Have been greatly blessed in trying, in some humble way, to share these labors with my companion. At times have been completely lifted out of self while standing before the congregation.

One evening, while pleading audibly at the altar, suddenly the whole church, and, to my vision, the streets of Moscow, seemed radiant with an unearthly, glorious light. 'Mid this light I beheld myself walking and crying, "Behold the Lamb!"

The next evening, while testifying for Jesus, in a wonderful, and to me hitherto unknown, manner, the Spirit came upon me, and I found myself walking the aisles of the church, entreating the unsaved to be reconciled to God, while hearts were melted before the voice of him who spake through the frail tenement of clay.

Being very weak in body, my husband afterward said that he feared the glory was more than I could endure; but I saw in it only another verification of "God hath chosen the foolish things of the world to confound the wise: and God hath chosen the weak things of the world to confound the things which are mighty;" and a fulfillment of the promise given me at the beginning of the year: "For ye shall go out with joy, and be led forth with peace; the mountains and the hills shall break forth before you into singing, and all the trees of the field shall clap their hands."

November 28th. The past few months have been months of trial. Mr. M'Allister's health failing, he was obliged, at last Conference, after nineteen years of itinerant life, to take a superannuated relation. None but those who have passed through the same trial, with heart still clinging to the work, know the cost of such a decision.

We were only partly settled in our home at Litchfield, when he was taken violently ill (hemorrhage of stomach), and for weeks seemed very near the close of earth's pilgrimage; but our Father in mercy has stooped again to the cry of stricken hearts, and he seems fast recovering.

January 1, 1870. A new year dawns upon us, and nestling in my arms I find a new-born babe.

> "This beautiful, mysterious thing,
>   This seeming visitant from heaven;
> This bird with the immortal wing,
>   To me, to me Thy hand has given.
> Doubts, hopes, in eager tumult rise;
>   Hear, O my God! one earnest prayer:
> Room for my bird in paradise,
>   And give his angel plumage there."

February 27th. Our Allie is nine years old to-day. For some time past, have been much drawn out in prayer for his speedy conversion. A short time since, unsolicited by any, he went *alone* to the altar of prayer, and, we think, gives good evidence of acceptance with God.

What a strange doctrine is that which would have our children wander for years in sin and folly, as a seeming necessity, and then be brought back to Christ! How much better to keep them always in the fold! The promise is to us and to our children.

October 10*th.* The experiences of the past Summer have been somewhat peculiar. From care of our little Eddie, have been much deprived of the public means of grace; but my mind has been strangely exercised regarding public work. For years, I have fully believed that to the women of the Church has been given a special mission for the Master, and that the promise of the Father, and its results, embraced both sexes, for "in Christ there is neither male nor female;" but have always had a strong, natural aversion to any thing that might be considered boldness in this direction. In the experiences of the past, I have been pressed, by what I fully believe to be the Spirit of God, to duties which, according to my previously formed opinions, were in direct opposition to the rules of female propriety; and, in the experiences of the present, I am constantly hearing, as it were, a voice saying, "I have set before thee an open door, and no man can shut it!" In communion with my Father in heaven, the word "appointment" is much before me, and I see myself standing in this and that place, warning sinners to flee from the wrath to come, and urging the Church to purity. At times I am inclined to think this all of the adversary, to hinder and distress me in my journey.

Last Sabbath, went with husband to his appointment at Sand Creek, but had no sooner taken my seat near the center of the church, than my mind became much exercised with the conviction that I had there some special duty, and this exercise of mind continued during the sermon, so that I trembled much in body, the words being pressed upon my heart: "If ye be willing and obedient, ye shall eat of the good of the land; but if ye be disobedient and rebel, the blood of souls will I require at your hands!"

Being thus impelled, I arose, at the close of the sermon, and asked the privilege of speaking; and as I gave utterance, as the Spirit led, unconsciously walked to the front of the altar, where I found myself when I ceased. A sweet consciousness of the approval of the Master, "She hath done what she could," followed this. But why these out-of-the-way duties? I find myself often asking.

December 20*th.* Our Woman's Foreign Missionary movement is inspiring the hearts and filling the hands of some of the sisters upon our (Albion) District.

I see in it the opening of a great door, and effectual. God's providence and Spirit is surely leading. I start back, almost appalled, in view of the responsibility. The ladies of our district have formed an association, of which I have been made a corresponding secretary, and informed that it is expected of me that I do what I can in the holding of public meetings, organizing societies, etc.

Went, recently, to Mosherville (my first "appointment"), and tried to talk for our cause; but thought most of the time, while speaking, that the congregation would be so glad when I had ended, and I *knew* I should. Would have been glad if there had been a passage back of the altar for going out, instead of passing down the aisle. Brother Mosher came to me with words of encouragement, asking if this was my first missionary address. I replied, "Yes: *and my last !*" for at that moment I felt that I could never again thus stand before the congregation.

August 24*th.* Our Albion Camp-meeting has just closed. To me it was a memorable season.

I had but just reached the ground, when a warmhearted brother grasped my hand, with the salutation: "I understand you preached at Spring Arbor last Sabbath. Sorry I was not there," etc. His words greatly distressed and tried me, and I thought to myself, if this is the report that is to go out from my little missionary talks, that "Sister M. has gone to preaching!" I will cease.

That evening, while kneeling in the congregation, asking for some promise upon which to rest my soul, this was given: "I can do all things through Christ who strengtheneth me."

A public missionary meeting had been announced, but as the ladies we had expected were not present, the lot to speak fell upon me; so I found that my time for *"ceasing"* had not yet come, unless, like Jonah, I ran from duty.

At the close of the missionary meeting, our pastor, Rev. G. W. Tuthill, came to our tent, and without there ever having a word passed between us on the subject, informed me that he expected to bring my case before the next quarterly-conference (which was to be in less than a week), as a candidate for license to preach. By his words I was thrown into great distress and perplexity of mind, and hastened to a retired part of the grove, where I spent most of the remainder of the day in tears and supplications, alone with God.

The next morning, in the closing scene of the meeting, while marching round the ground, as I took the hand of Rev. N. L. Brockway, in a moment's time, I seemed lifted above earth into the presence of our departed. The glory of that hour is indescribable.

I could not move a step farther, nor could I utter a word. The next I was conscious of, I was resting in the arms of my dear sisters, while the songs of Zion filling the air, the shouts of praise, the countenances of God's saints, and all nature around, seemed heavenly beyond description.

That night, after returning home, I awoke, at the midnight hour, with the words, "Go ye into all the world, and preach the Gospel to every creature," with a peculiar emphasis upon "ye." My room seemed lighted up with the glory of God. I arose in my bed, and said, audibly, "I'll go, Lord;" for at that moment the way seemed clear. But in the morning it was thrust aside as nothing more than a vision of the night.

Whatever the Master would have me do, I can see no necessity for a formal license; but believe it would be a hinderance, instead of help, to my work; and in this my husband and others concur.

September 2d. Spent some time in conversasion with brother Tuthill to-day. He still presses the license question, bringing some seemingly strong arguments in favor; yet I think there are as many against.

He desires me to speak here next Sabbath evening. I told him that, if he wished a missionary meeting, I would do the best I could, but could take no farther responsibility.

Am greatly distressed in mind. O God, undertake for me! I would do thy will; but this *can not* be my duty.

September 4th. Spoke at the missionary meeting last evening, to a full house; but felt little freedom or satisfaction in my work.

I seem to be enshrouded in darkness. The words, "Go ye," follow me. They meet me in the closet, in the class-room, in the prayer-circle, and in the great congregation. "Whither shall I go from thy Spirit; or whither shall I flee from thy presence?" And yet I have loved to go at the bidding of the Master. But he requires no impossibility.

November 5th. Have decided to go forward. My mind is sweetly stayed upon Christ.

Perhaps I need this crucifixion, for my own

good. It is much pressed upon my mind that I must begin my work at home.

November 10*th.* Have had conversation with our present pastor, Rev. W. H. Ware, as I felt that I could not, and ought not to, speak upon his charge without his approval.

He, too, presses the license question, and again I am thrown into perplexity. "License to preach!" is not what I want. I only want to work and talk for Jesus as he bids me. I am not willing the report should go before me, "She has license to preach."

I fully believe—such are the prejudices of the Church and world—it would hinder my usefulness, in that so much more would be expected. I can not consent.

What I have suffered in mind, for the past few days, God only knows.

January 3, 1872. Went, on last Saturday, by invitation of the pastor (Rev. J. Clubine), with husband, to North Adams, to spend Sabbath and attend watch-meeting.

It was a season of blessed experience to my soul. Felt much depression of mind on my way there, and much shrinking in view of the cross, but was lifted above all; and, in an unusual manner, God's Spirit was poured out upon his people.

February 28*th.* We have just returned from a week's stay at Union City, spent in labor for souls. God greatly helped; and we were permitted to see some precious souls come to Christ, and some of the leaders in Zion come out in clear, definite testimony regarding the efficacy of the Blood to cleanse from all sin. Never before was I enabled so fully and constantly to rest upon the promise, "Lo, I am with you alway."

July 10*th.* The past four months have been a season of great conflict with the powers of darkness. At times, feel to cry out, "My God! my God! why hast thou forsaken me?"

Find in my heart a great aversion of feeling to any public work. Have been greatly pressed, and almost constantly occupied, with my household cares. I am in the midst of these, placed here by Providence, and God's order is always one of perfect harmony. One duty never interferes with another.

Yet, at times, find myself in much conflict of mind. Have settled the question of public work thus: I will try and meet all the demands of

God's providence in this direction. Will go to the ends of the earth with my companion, if God calls, trying in every way to hold up his hands; and will labor as God opens the way, both in public and private, for the upbuilding of his cause; but will avoid every thing that looks like the assuming of *special* public work. May I not in this way fully meet the requirement, "Go ye into all the world and preach the Gospel?" for preaching, in its generic sense, means simply "a proclaiming of the love of Christ to a lost and ruined world."

Mr. M'Allister hopes to be able to take work at the next session of Conference. To this I am looking forward with earnest longing. Have felt, of late, that most willingly would I spend my life in going from house to house, in talking and praying with the people, if I may but be released from this one cross constantly before me.

Recently attended a missionary meeting at Jackson, but felt no freedom in speaking; but, on the contrary, was filled with anguish, the moment I had ceased, in the thought that God's cause had not been honored.

August 22d. Our Albion Camp-meeting for this year has just ended. What a year of conflict the past has been! But, God be praised, I have not been left comfortless. During this meeting I enjoyed much of His presence.

Here I asked that, if it were the Lord's will that I enter more fully into work for the Master, some person might be given me with whom I might safely leave the care of my family during my absence from home. Again and again, after making this request, Miss H. Melvin, a Christian lady from Adrian, then on the ground, though a stranger to me, was presented to my mind as the person; but such were her circumstances that I thought it impossible, and said nothing.

After our return, we were surprised by a visit from her, and her remark that she felt that she could not return to Adrian without first coming to our home; and that, the moment she crossed our threshold, she felt as though a hand was laid heavily upon her.

Before leaving, she decided, if the way opened, to meet us at Conference, and go with us to our field of labor, wherever it might be.

Am much drawn out in prayer that God will direct our steps; that, if not for his glory, if we may be more useful in promiscuous work, the way may not open for us to take regular work. We rest in the promise: "In all thy ways acknowledge Him, and he shall direct thy paths." "He shall choose our inheritance for us."

Earthly considerations have no power to influence our hearts; but we feel, more and more, that the one work of soul-saving must be ours.

I remarked, in one of our social gatherings near the close of this camp-meeting, that I expected to know in the future, as I had not known in the past, the meaning of "Alone with Jesus." Wondered, as I took my seat, why I thus expressed myself; but felt that, in some way, the words had a deep significance.

My experience is not as satisfactory as in the past. Have not that constant abiding by faith in Christ, and joy in believing, I once possessed. But I believe I shall yet praise Him "who is the help of my countenance." I call to mind the past, when I said, My foot slippeth; but the mercy of the Lord held me up.

August 27th. Spent last Sabbath at Hanover. It was a Sabbath of sweet rest to my soul. Husband preached from "Be filled with the Spirit." God wonderfully helped in the utterances of that hour, as he placed before the Church her blessed privileges in this respect, and the glorious results of being thus filled with the Spirit of our living Head.

In the evening, held a missionary meeting, at which I spoke for a short time.

September 15th. Husband has been very poorly for several weeks past. Is now very sick. Was to have preached at the Congregational Church to-day (has for some time been occasionally supplying that pulpit). Had announced for his theme, "Entire Consecration," and has been very anxious to be able to meet his engagement.

September 20th. Husband is still very low. It has been a week of great anxiety. Conference is now in session at Jackson. Had looked forward with much anticipation to the meeting with loved ones in Christ on that occasion. The words,

> "God moves in a mysterious way,
> His wonders to perform,"

are much on my mind.

September 23d. Watching still, night and day, by the bedside of my suffering companion. A line from Miss H. Melvin this evening, saying that she will be here on the morning train. She had expected to meet us at Conference.

During the night, my mind was much exercised with the words, "Behold the fire and the wood; but where is the lamb for a burnt-offering? And Abraham said, My son, God will provide himself a lamb for a burnt-offering?"

All seems shrouded in mystery and darkness. See by the papers that we have no appointment. Find our hearts were much set on again entering the effective ranks; but, on my knees, I have been enabled to thank God for all the dispensations of his providence, *both joyous and afflictive.*

September 29th. Hattie Melvin is with us. *Sent of the Lord,* seems best to express her mission to us. Being a practical nurse, she seems just what we now most need.

Husband seems slowly improving; but is still very weak.

October 3d. Mr. M'Allister is able to sit up but very little. I gain no evidence in prayer regarding his recovery. When pleading in this direction, these words are invariably applied to my mind, "I was brought low, and he helped me." I can not comprehend them. Clouds and darkness seem gathered about us. At times, am filled with foreboding fears; then, again, am lifted above all. Husband is very hopeful, and physicians give much encouragement.

October 28th. How unsearchable are the judgments of God, and "his ways past finding out!" "For who hath known the mind of the

Lord, or who hath been his counselor?" "I was brought low, and he helped me!"

Three weeks ago, my dear companion seemed fast recovering, when suddenly he was prostrated by a nervous chill, and, in a few hours, his mind became an entire wreck. His physician expressed but little hope of his ever being any better, as his little remaining strength was only kept up by the constant use of stimulant. God only knows the anguish of those hours.

Near six P. M., as I was sitting watching by his side, suddenly, as if a voice were speaking, the question was presented, "If your husband live, will you, from this hour, take upon you this cross, that of preaching my Gospel?" Unprepared to answer, I thrust it from me. Soon after, his physician coming in, in reply to my anxious questioning, and the entreaty that he would keep nothing from me, as it were better that I knew the worst and prepare for it, gave me to understand that there was but little, if any, chance for hope. Anguish indescribable filled my soul at the thought of the bitter cup before me; but one thought seemed to penetrate my being as none other—that of going *alone* to labor in the vineyard of the Master; and then he, on whom I had so heavily leaned, passing away without one word of parting counsel or comfort.

Near eleven, with still greater emphasis, the question again came, "If your husband recover, will you, from this hour, take upon you this cross, and obey the command, 'Go ye into all the world and preach the Gospel?'" Fearful was the struggle; but there, seemingly standing with earth's dearest friend upon the very brink of the river of death, I entered into a solemn covenant with God, that, let the consequences be what they would regarding this life, from that hour that cross should be mine.

In a moment, all anxiety regarding my husband was lifted from me, and I could have shouted aloud the praises of my Deliverer; and with this came the assurance that at twelve his mind would return. Precisely at the midnight hour, his mind began to rally, and before one, he was himself again.

A few hours after, having lain down to get some rest, there came up before my mind a view like this: I saw my companion and myself standing upon the brink of the river of death. All was midnight darkness about the river, the waters of which were perfectly smooth, not a ripple being discernible.

On the river I could discern, notwithstanding the darkness, different small boats; and each boatman, with muffled oar, seemed anxiously watching for the command to be given from the opposite shore, to come for my husband.

Then, on the opposite side of the river from where we were standing, there came a glorified band, among whom I realized the presence of *our* loved, departed ones come to welcome him. As I gazed upon this company of white-robed redeemed ones, my soul was filled with a glory no tongue can describe.

Then, as I glanced back to where we were standing, I saw myself, with my hand, waving the boatmen back; and as I thus stood, making every exertion to keep them from coming for husband, I saw the glorified company turn from the shore toward the celestial city, while my companion and myself turned toward earth. The rapture of this hour no mortal tongue can express; but I believe it to be a faint glimpse of what we shall feel when our life's work is wrought, and our friends welcome us to the city above.

November 18*th.* Husband has seemed in a very critical condition for the past three weeks. No one during this time has been permitted to enter his room but the family. Hattie Melvin and myself have had almost the entire care of him, as we dare not risk a change of watchers. He is wasted to a mere skeleton. Most of this time the village have been in hourly expectation of hearing the bell toll, announcing his departure to the land of rest; but I have felt clear in the assurance that he will again mingle in the family circle. He is too weak to converse much, but is calm and patient, some of the time triumphant. He fully expects to recover. Says that when again permitted to enter the vineyard of the Master, he will have a new experience from which to preach—that he shall preach holiness as never before.

November 20*th*. Mr. M'Allister is still improving. Am pressed in spirit with regard to a public confession regarding the convictions of the past two years. Feel that I dare not enter our church without; yet difficulties are in the way which seem insurmountable. Is this, *can this* be my duty? Am fully decided regarding the work itself, as the Lord opens the way; but would not such an act seem like the opening of the door for one's self? God, my Father, knows I would not go until sent, nor can I longer tarry if the Master *bids* me go. But my convictions seem so strange, so full of mystery to myself, so fully in opposition to all the prejudices of the past! What will they be to others?

November 24th. On yesterday, received a letter from sister Crawford, in which she says:

"God, my Father, reveals to me that he has something for you to do. I feel that either a *great duty* or a *great sorrow* hangs just over your head. I am with you every moment, waking or sleeping, and so drawn out in prayer for you.

"In my dreams, I am pressing you to the cross; awake in the silence of the night, with outstretched hands, pleading for you. God will lift up your head. He will hold you by the right-hand. He will be with your mouth, and teach you what to say. God is with thee! God thine everlasting light! O Emily, hear him say, 'Go forward!'"

Her words overwhelmed me, and, for hours, in a flood of tears I walked the house, crying, "If it be possible, let this cup pass from me;" but when I added, "Nevertheless, not my will but Thine be done," sweet peace filled my soul.

November 29th. Mr. M'Allister and myself have to-day had conversation with Rev. E. D. Young (our present pastor), in which I told him of the experience of the past, keeping nothing back. When I had ended, he said, "Let us ask direction of God before going farther."

Instead of asking for himself (I supposed that

what I had said had thrown him into perplexity of mind), he pleaded with God that every doubt might be removed from my mind, and I have strength to go forward in the work given me to do. My soul was richly baptized, and again I saw my way clear in the words, "*I have set before thee an open door!*"

December 2*d.* The cross I have so long tried to pass round, I have at last found strength (not my own) to move on before me. Went to church last evening, and told the story of the conflicts of the past and decision of the present. Some wondered, some wept, and this heart realized, as never before, the meaning of the words given me at Albion Camp-meeting: "*Alone with Jesus.*"

December 4*th.* The past three days have been such hours of conflict and crucifixion to the world as I have never before known. Yesterday, at morning-prayer, opened to "We have forsaken all, and followed Thee: what shall we have therefore?" I have entered upon the possession of my inheritance, and am satisfied. "In the world tribulation, but in Christ peace." With this cross I am being lifted toward my crown. Ah, the nearer I get to Calvary, the smaller my cross appears! How it dwindles into insignificance!

Last evening, while met in our social-meeting, in telling my brethren and sisters in Christ that my trust was in the God of Israel, a rich baptism rested upon me, and if, instead of a small congregation of Christ's disciples, I had had before me the multitude of opposing men and women, I am sure I could have spoken unto them Jesus and the resurrection.

December 5th. Husband continues to improve. Has rode out some this week. Yesterday, we visited at the parsonage. A large company present. He enjoyed it much. Three months since his last visit. We are beginning to anticipate very soon being able to redeem our pledges made to several, to assist in extra meetings during the Winter.

December 10th. On yesterday, husband was able to be about the street attending to his business. My heart was filled with joy and gratitude; but this morning he was taken suddenly worse. His physician expresses fears concerning him, which, from kindness to me, he has not before mentioned. I can not but think he will soon be better again.

Rev. E. D. Young and brother Kellog (class-leader) have spent the evening with him. Had a blessed season of prayer. Husband was very triumphant. After they left, he called me to his side, saying: " My dear, does it not do your soul good to hear persons pray with such access to the Throne? Did you notice how confidently they asked that I might 'yet preach Christ as never in the past?'"

December 12*th.* O, what hours are these! All yesterday, hope seemed giving way to fear. Last evening, my dear friend, Mrs. Rev. H. Jordan (formerly Mrs. Twogood) very unexpectedly came to me. Did not God, my Father, see my need, and send her to strengthen my falling hands? We prayed together for husband. Blessed access was given. O, how I was pressed to the bosom of Infinite Love, until I asked for his life, when suddenly, my mouth was closed, and I could not utter a sentence more!

This morning, the certainty of the future seems settling upon me. *Alone* I seem to stand, exposed to the pelting storm, while, one after another, every earthly prop is being taken away.

They have just been singing by his bedside, "The war is almost ended now!" *He* exults; *I* weep! O, what anguish; what desolation! And not one gleam of light!

> "Deep in unfathomable mines
> Of never-failing skill,
> He treasures up his bright designs,
> And works his sovereign will."

CHAPTER XI.

DECEMBER 18TH. *It is past;* and I sit down in my desolated home, not to write of pain and anguish, but of joy and victory!

"Life hath won the victory—
Trodden death beneath his feet!"

On Thursday, the twelfth, we were convinced that an ulcer had broken in the left lung of my husband, and that we could not longer hope for his recovery. Upon being informed of his situation, with a smile he replied, "It is all right; *I am all ready!*"

Friday afternoon, we saw that he was failing fast. Toward night, he said, "Pray that if it be the Lord's will, I may have strength given me to talk to each, separately." This prayer seemed immediately answered, and he commenced giving to weeping ones, at his bedside, such words of parting counsel as will always be remembered.

He spoke in holy triumph of his recent, last conflict with the powers of darkness; of the power given him to say to the tempter, as he came with his accusations, "Thus far shalt thou come, and no farther;" saying that, as he uttered these words, he "saw the Lord Jesus standing right behind him," and then he knew he was conqueror. During all that night of intense suffering, his face beamed with an unearthly radiance; and such were the utterances constantly falling from his lips, so full of glory the responses given, as the songs of Zion, such as

"I know I am nearing the holy ranks,"

"Shall we gather at the river,"

"Rock of Ages, cleft for me,"

etc., were sung in his room, that all who entered felt the import of the words:

"The place where the good man meets his fate
Is privileged beyond the common walks
Of virtuous life, quite on the verge of heaven."

At midnight, during a severe paroxysm of pain, we thought him going; but he soon rallied, and from that hour he seemed more like a resident of the glorified land than of this vale of tears.

To my father and mother, he spoke of the conflicts and victories of the past; of the trial of not being permitted, on account of failing health, to remain in the regular work; of the precious labor in which he had been permitted to engage during his superannuated relation, that of going here and there presenting Christ a perfect Savior; of the little heart he had had for worldly engagements; of the all-consuming love of the soul for the Church, and of the little he had accomplished; but exulted in the consciousness that the merits of Christ covered all the deficiencies of his life.

Then he spoke of the custom, when the country was new, of the father of the family going to what was then the Far West, to make ready the new home; of the parting, and joyful anticipation with which the separated family looked forward to the reunion around their own hearth-stone. Then, of himself as only going a little ahead of us; of the joy with which he should welcome us as, one after another, we crossed over the river for the eternal reunion in our Father's house above.

Then, with a smile upon his face, he turned to me, as I was sitting near the foot of his bed, saying, "And now, if Emily will only let me go cheerfully, I am all ready!" In anguish of soul, I threw myself by his side, exclaiming, "I *will* let you go, my dear; only speak a few more words of comfort to your poor Emily!" Instead of being moved by my sorrow, those who looked upon him say, unutterable glory shone upon his face as, throwing his arms about me, he replied: "My precious one, you have a work to do for the Master! You will have *crosses*, you will have conflicts, you will have reproaches; but O, the reward! O, the reward! Will you do that work? *Will you do it?*"

Upon my replying, "In the strength of Israel's God, I will!" "Glory! glory! Halleluiah! Victory! victory.!" burst from his lips for some time. Then, turning to those around (Rev. E. D. Young and brother Kellog being present), in burning words, he commended his soon-to-be-widowed one to the sympathy and help of the Church.

On the morning of the fourteenth, he fixed his eye upon a window near the foot of his bed, intently gazing, as if upon some object in the distance, while a smile of rapture overspread his countenance. Hattie Melvin asked, "What do you see, brother M'Allister?" He replied, "Do you see any thing unusual?" She said, "No: but you do; what is it?" By this time, I had reached his side, and said, "What *do* you see?" "Had I strength and language, I would tell you," he replied. "Can't you give us just a *hint* of what you see?" Upon his lips being moistened, he said, "My Father! my Father! the chariot and the horsemen!" and, with enraptured eye and shining countenance, continued gazing.

Soon after, upon Dr. Howard's coming into his room, he exultantly asked: "What do you think of my case *now*, Doctor? Do you think you can keep me now?" Then, as he took the parting hand of his faithful physician, "Are you going home now, Doctor?" An affirmative reply being given, he said, "You will get home first; but I shall get my mansion first!"

He then requested us to pray. I repeated his request to brother Kellog, who replied, "I do not feel at all like praying; I feel more like praising!" to which he replied, "That will do a great deal better!" When brother Kellog had ceased, my beloved made known to me that he wished me to follow; and there, on the margin of the river of death, I gave back to God his own, until we meet at the marriage-supper of the Lamb.

Several unconverted coming in as we arose from our knees, in a whisper he commenced exhorting them to come to Christ; and did not cease until they had promised to give their hearts to God, and meet him in heaven. He then desired that we should go to prayer for these, which was done.

Soon after, brother Young said, "Brother M'Allister, have you a word of parting to send to your brethren at Conference?" He immediately replied: "Tell my brethren I have been connected with the Conference twenty-one years. They have been years of toil and trouble; and sometimes I have thought, Why may not I turn aside as well as others, and seek wealth and ease? But now I understand it! Now I see my reward! *I am rich enough now!* If I may give my advice, never turn aside from the work to which God has called you; but be faithful. Preach Christ! Preach holiness! *Never be ashamed of it!*"

At near eleven A. M., he requested to be raised in bed. This being accomplished, we saw that a great change had come over him, and that he was swiftly passing to the land which knows no suffering.

He was unable longer to speak, even in a whisper; but we had agreed to hold each other's hand until the last moment, and, if unable to speak, a pressure was to be the signal that all was light, all glorious about the river.

I pause; for no pen can describe the glory which now seemed filling the room, resting upon the face, and lighting up the countenance of the sufferer.

One after another of the sweet songs of Zion were sung by those around, each one wafting, as on downy wing, nearer and nearer the open portal of glory, from whence the light was streaming and resting upon the face of clay.

As for myself, although my heart was being riven with anguish, I seemed not only permitted in song to follow his flight, but my spirit seemed almost to keep pace with his, as it gazed upon the glories of the unseen.

As they were singing,

> "Out of my stony griefs
> Bethel I'll raise:
> So by my woes to be
> Nearer, my God, to thee,
> Nearer to thee!"

by repeated pressures of the hand, he gave me to understand that he knew they were singing that hymn for me. Then his eye became fixed, and for about an hour he was unconscious to all around. Brother Young remarked, "He is forever beyond our reach now!" Dr. Howard, holding his pulse, said, "He is almost gone!" and I had ceased to look longer for the sign of recognition until, with my work done, we should meet again on the farther shore.

Some one said, "Sing; he possibly may hear, even though we know it not."

They commenced singing, "My sins are washed away in the blood of the Lamb;" and, as they came to the words, "Death is overcome through the blood of the Lamb," Hattie Melvin said, "O see, sister M'Allister! he is looking at you." I replied, "Why, Hattie, you know he can not see us [he had previously told us that he could not see];" but soon felt a slight pressure of the hand, and bent over him with the inquiry, "Can you see me, my dear?" to which he replied in the affirmative. "Is there any thing you want? Can we do any thing for you?" in reply to which, with some difficulty, he gave us to understand that he wished to be laid back upon the bed. This being done, the death-like expression all passed from his eyes, and, instead, they sparkled with unearthly beauty and light; and, for a moment, I thought, as did others, Perhaps God is yet going to raise him up to preach Christ.

"The blood! the blood! Victory! victory!" then burst from his lips, after which he made a great effort to speak, as if wishing to communicate something to me. I asked: "Is there any thing you wish to say to us? Have you come back to finish up your work?" Immediately an affirmative response (by the moving of the lips, the nod of the head, and the pressure of the hand) was given. "What is it?" A great effort to speak. "Have you seen the loved ones?" "Yes."* "Have you seen Katie?" "Yes." "Have you seen Joey?" "Yes." "Have you seen Truman?" "Yes." "Have you seen the other loved ones?" "Yes." "Is this what you came back to tell us?" "No." "What *is* it, then?" Again there was a great effort to speak, and I asked, "Is it any thing special to me?" "Yes." "Is it any thing concerning my work?" A look of satisfaction, showing that I had at last reached the right question, now beamed from his face as he replied, with much emphasis, "Yes." Overwhelmed with wonder, I hesitated, when brother Young said, "Sister M'Allister, ask him if your convictions regarding your life-work are correct?" I repeated the question, to which he quickly responded, "Yes." "Is *this* what you came back to tell us?" "Yes." "Will I have strength to go forward?" "Yes."

I then said to those around: "He will go now very quick. *His work is done!*" To which he responded, with unutterable glory in his look, "Yes." Brother Young then turned to me and said, "Sister M'Allister, have you any doubts *now* regarding your duty?" Upon my replying, "No:

* These responses were all given by the same triple sign.

in the strength of Elijah's God, I'll go!" "Victory! victory!" again burst from his lips, in which I joined; and upon my strength giving way, they laid me upon the bed beside him, and, for a moment, I knew not but that together we were to be permitted to enter the open gate.

Then said one, standing by, "Look! O look! he is trying to clap his hands!" I raised myself and assisted him in his last work upon earth, several times clapping his hands together in token of victory. Then, without moving a muscle, and not a sigh or groan—only the victory on the lips and the clasped hands—the spirit entered into rest. A thin veil separated us, while I turned *alone* toward earth, clasping to my heart the standard of the cross fallen from his nerveless grasp.

They have buried my dead out of my sight. "He being dead, yet speaketh!"

O, now I see why he was permitted to turn with me from the dark river toward life's work. I thought it to have been for a longer time; but God, my Father, knoweth best. I, too, have seen the answer to the prayer of which my beloved spake so confidently, that he might yet "*preach Christ as never in the past!*" O, what a sermon was that preached on his dying bed!

We carried him to his last resting-place just

as the sun was sinking behind the western hills. A halo of glory overspread the sky, and I thought, Thus has his earthly sun gone down! Then, as I entered our desolated home and looked from an eastern window, the full moon was rising in all its grandeur. Ah, such is the immortal life upon which he has entered!

December 19*th*. Last evening was a season of severe conflict with the cruel adversary of all righteousness, he constantly suggesting that, in order that I be fully prepared for my work, all my earthly comforts would soon be stripped from me; that my children, too, would be lain away in the grave; my home burned; and, in every sense of the word, I would become a wanderer, daylight all gone, and darkness forever over me!

The fierce storm was raging without; earthly protector gone, and, with feelings only known to those who have passed through the same, I laid my body down to rest, and at last slept; but was soon awakened by what seemed a voice repeating the words of the Psalm (xci) read at the memorial service of my dear husband: "He shall cover thee with his feathers, and under his wings shalt thou trust. Thou shalt not be afraid for the terror by night; nor for the arrow that flieth by day. For he shall give his angels charge over thee, to keep thee in all thy ways. They shall bear thee up in their hands, lest thou dash thy foot against a stone. Thou shalt tread upon the lion and the adder: the young lion and the dragon shalt thou trample under foot."

December 20th. Our little Eddie is three years old to-day. He goes about the house, saying, "My papa up in the sky, called me his precious little lamb, and said I must be a good boy." He often asks us to sing, "Shall we gather at the river." After singing it to-day, he threw his arms around the neck of Ella and Allie, saying, "This is what we'll do when we gather at the riber!" Precious one! he little realizes his great loss.

A letter to-day from my dear friend, sister Crawford. She has just learned of the departure of my dear one to the mansions above, and says:

"O Emily, what a night I have passed! Hour after hour I lay upon my couch, my soul in deepest, closest sympathy with yours. You seemed near me. Some of the time my arms were encircling you. Some of the time you were kneeling at my feet, resting your weary head upon my lap, while my lips were trying to pour words of comfort into your heart. Is it possible my frail tender plant again stands *alone*, exposed to the rough blasts of earth? Could I have known this

Saturday, should have come to you instead of stopping here [Battle Creek].

"O, my precious Emily, do not let your faith waver for one moment! I think I see, in part, dimly perhaps, but our God 'moves in a mysterious way his wonders to perform.' Move on, thou mighty Jehovah! Only give us grace to say, '*Thy will be done?*'

"I spent yesterday afternoon with sisters Smith and Mosher. Soon after we were seated in the parlor, sister Smith said, 'Brother Joy was here to dinner, and said brother M'Allister is buried to-day.' I was so shocked and bewildered I could scarcely utter a word.

"A few nights before I left home, I had been awakened by a voice saying, 'Your precious friend's husband is dead.' I awoke husband, and told him of what seemed to be spoken. He said, 'I fear brother M'Allister is not going to stay long!' It seemed like the voice of brother Gregory, at whose house I am now stopping. He was sitting on the sofa by my side when sister Smith spoke of the burial."

Brother Crawford thus writes me: "I'll venture the assertion, if you and I could have stood close by the bank on this side the river, we should have heard his shouts as they came echoing back across the river, and instead of weeping at the thought that he had left you, you would have caught the hallowed flame, and your voice would have reached his ear upon the other shore, and it would have been glory here, and glory there."

Ah yes: and thus it was! I heard his shouts, and caught the hallowed flame, and my voice reached his ear as he stepped upon the other shore, and it *was* "glory here, and glory there!"

December 28th. Two weeks ago, to-day, since our home was so honored by the coming of the "Chariot of Israel and the horsemen thereof," bearing from thence the spirit of one of Christ's chosen embassadors. A sacred influence still lingers in his room. He seems not far away!

Brother Young has just been here. He wishes me to speak in our church to-morrow evening. I am ready to follow my Guide. He leadeth me.

December 30th. Spoke last evening, from "These are they which follow the Lamb whithersoever he goeth." Was kept calm and collected. In this I am a wonder to myself.

January 1, 1873. Another year past, and its records in eternity.

"Days come and go, in joy or woe;
Days come and go, in endless sum.

> Only the eternal day
>   Shall come, but never go;
> Only the eternal tide
>   Shall never ebb, but flow.
> O, long eternity,
> My soul goes forth to thee!"

Our watch-meeting was a season of refreshing from the presence of the Lord. For myself, anew I realized the depth of meaning in the words of an apostle: "For ye are not come unto the mount that might be touched, and that burned with fire; nor unto blackness and darkness and tempest. But ye are come unto Mount Zion, and unto the city of the living God, the heavenly Jerusalem, and to an innumerable company of angels."

January 7th. Last week was the Week of Prayer. The three Churches of our place came unitedly to the mercy-seat, and realized a precious outpouring of the Spirit.

The Baptist minister came out in clear, definite testimony of the efficacy of the blood to cleanse. Great power rested upon him. His words were greatly blessed to my soul. O, when shall Zion's watchmen all awake and put on their strength?

On Saturday, just before the close of evening service, brother Young came to me, with the united request from the pastors that I speak in our Church on Sabbath evening; saying that, if I would consent, there would be no services in the other churches. My hand was in that of my unseen Guide, and I dared not refuse.

In a moment after, the Congregationalist minister came, with the request that I speak in his church instead of ours, to which I consented, when I remembered the last and unfilled appointment of my now sainted companion, and immediately felt that his must be *my* theme for the coming evening.

On returning from morning service, no preparation as yet having been made for the evening, I retired to the study, and, in a flood of tears, walked the room, pleading with God that, if he had called me to this work, the needed help might be given. My eye rested upon my dear one's pocket Bible, the companion of years as he went here and there preaching Christ. I hastily took it, clasping it to my heart, and then opened to where a leaf was turned down to the words, "If we walk in the light as he is in the light, we have fellowship one with another, and the blood of Jesus Christ his Son cleanseth us from all sin;" and in them saw my way clear for the evening.

Realized a lifting up above the fear of man as I tried to present Christ, a perfect Savior, to the large congregation, many, no doubt, having come from mere curiosity.

"I shall meet all these again at the judgment-bar of God," was so impressed upon my mind, that, for the time, the strangeness of my position was forgotten.

But, O how strange, how mysterious, that such a worm should be called to such a work! If at the great day one soul may but be found upon the right-hand that otherwise would have been on the left, the mystery will be solved, and my reward sure.

February 14th. The extra meetings, commenced at the Week of Prayer, still continue. Six weeks of earnest work, resulting in a great quickening of the Church, and the salvation of many precious souls, have passed. Among the newly saved are several of the leading business men of our place. To God be all the glory!

Most of my time has been spent in these meetings, and in personal effort for souls. Have been permitted to see several, for whom my soul has long been burdened, brought into the fold of Christ. In fact, I find so much to do in the vineyard, that I have no time to sit idly by the way, brooding over my sorrow; and, although God has seen fit, in his providence, to hang over my path the cloud that of all others I bewailed, at times I see it as a pillar of fire moving on before me.

By invitation of the pastors, spent several days at Jackson, and one at Mosherville. God here helped me to raise the standard of the Cross.

Have had some conflicts of late. A few days since, a paper giving me license to exhort was handed me by my pastor; and on Saturday last I was requested to be present at the Quarterly Conference, to pass the usual examination as a candidate for license to preach.

All my prejudices and self-will in this direction I am trying to lay at the feet of Jesus.

> "If Thy grace vouchsafe to use
> The meanest of thy creatures, me,
> The time, the deed, the manner, choose."

February 16*th*. The work here still goes on. The Church is putting on her beautiful attire, and going forth to glorious victory.

Tried to speak, on Sabbath evening, to a large congregation gathered in our Church; but, not feeling usual freedom of spirit, the adversary took the advantage, and yesterday was passed in severe trial and conflict. It seemed utterly impossible to go another step forward in the path marked out for me; and the new and peculiar relation sustained to the Church pressed heavily upon me.

O, how I missed the words of comfort and encouragement I have been wont to hear in such seasons of trial! I almost longed for the grave to cover my defenseless head. A place beside my dear husband looked the most inviting spot upon earth.

In the night, I was awakened, as on a previous occasion, over a year since, with the words, " Go ye into all the world ;" but this time with the emphasis on " *Go;*" and " Lo, I am with you alway." The cloud was lifted, and again I rested upon the arm of my Beloved.

February 20*th*. Am now at St. Joseph, with my dear friends, brother and sister Crawford, where I came, by invitation of brother Crawford, to do what little I can for the Master. Find souls here seeking Christ. The Lord greatly helped, last evening, in speaking for him.

I have for some time looked forward to this meeting with my dear sister Crawford, as a means of comfort and strength. God, my Father, in tenderness, hath granted me the desire of my heart. The journey here, on yesterday, was a sad one ; for my husband and myself had anticipated coming together.

March 3d. Still at St. Joseph. Have been permitted to see some precious souls—among these an interesting class of young ladies—come to Christ.

Yesterday morning, lifted a heavy cross, in standing before the congregation in this land of strangers; but was sustained by grace divine.

Last evening was spent, by invitation of the pastor, Rev. H. Worthington, at Benton Harbor.

Here I found the largest congregation gathered I ever stood before, and but two or three familiar faces. One thought seemed constantly with me: We meet for the first, and probably for the last time, until the great gathering, when to the righteous it shall be said, "Come, ye blessed of my Father, inherit the kingdom prepared for you from the foundation of the world;" but to the wicked, "Depart from me, ye cursed, into everlasting fire, prepared for the devil and his angels."

Heaven seemed very near, as I told them of the triumphant death of my dear companion.

Much revival interest has been manifest here for some time. Several new ones arose, last evening, for prayer.

Nearly two weeks have been spent with my dear brother and sister Crawford in sweet fellowship and labor with God's dear people in this place. The time of separation will soon come; but we'll meet again.

Find it a trial to be separated from my family, but in cheering power the words are oft applied: "Leave thy fatherless children with me: I will preserve them alive ;" and regarding all temporal interests, I rest confidently upon the promise which has been given me several times in the experience of the past: "But my God shall supply all your need according to his riches in glory by Christ Jesus."

Sister Crawford has to-day given me some items of her past experience. With her permission, I here record them, believing they will be blessed to others as to me.

EXPERIENCE OF FULL SALVATION.

"At the age of twelve, I gave my heart to God and my name to the Church. For years I walked, sometimes in the light and sometimes in doubt and darkness. At the age of thirty-four, through the labors of a faithful class-leader, Dr. J. B. Tuttle, of Jackson, Michigan, I was brought to feel my need of a clean heart, and to see my privilege as never before. Several weeks I struggled, fasted, and prayed, and, at times, in anguish of spirit cried, 'Victory or death!' The struggle was severe; but victory was mine through the Conqueror.

"At the close of a day of unceasing prayer, I kneeled at my bedside, feeling that *all* was placed upon the altar, and yet fearing that the flaming eye of Jehovah saw that the consecration was not *entire*. I said, 'Show me, dear Father, wherein I lack, or what withhold?' Immediately the question was asked, 'If the Lord should take your husband from earth, would you be submissive?' With tears and anguish of soul, I said, 'Yes: I'll step out upon this broad earth alone, if it be Thy will!' 'Will you go forth and labor for the salvation of souls, talk and pray with sinners?' My heart and my flesh shrank, but cried, 'Any thing; only receive me, fully save me!' In an instant these words were given: 'And ye shall seek me, and find me, when ye shall search for me with all your heart. And I will be found of you, saith the Lord.' My soul replied, It is enough.

> "'T is done, the great transaction's done;
> I am my Lord's, and he is mine!'

My burden gone, I arose and lay me down to sleep without any joyous emotion, but resting, trusting, fully in the promise, 'I will be found of thee!'

"I slept, and dreamed that I was in the midst

of a broad river, its waters clear as crystal. There seemed to be logs, placed one against the other, upon which I was walking. Just ahead of me were a few dear followers of Jesus, as it appeared, hastening to a temple in a beautiful grove far in the distance. I could see a narrow path leading up the embankment to the temple we were so eager to gain. The opposite side of the stream appeared low and marshy. A few dear sisters were following me. To my surprise, I came to a place where one log was removed, and asked, 'What shall I do?' They could not advise. Knowing that husband was on shore, I called, saying, 'Just one log gone; what shall I do?' He, waving his hand, replied, 'Plunge in, my dear; it won't harm you!'

"With perfect confidence, I stepped into the pure stream. It did not overflow me; but I was made every whit whole. The glory that filled my soul soon awoke me, and 'lo, God was in the place!' For days I walked and talked with him.

> 'Not a cloud did arise to darken my skies,
> Or hide for a moment my Lord from my eyes.'

But the enemy of all righteousness was dissatisfied with this; and, though kept at bay for a time, came in like a flood. But, thank God, the Spirit of the Lord lifted up a standard against him. Hidden in the cleft of the Rock, I was safe. In this hiding-place I keep me, and am safe still. Not I, but Jesus keeps me!

"'Forever here my rest shall be,
Close to thy bleeding side!'

"VIEW OF THE CROSS.

"Six years ago last Winter, feeling that special duties were laid upon me, my whole nature shrank. The cross seemed too heavy. Two days and one night I prayed to be excused.

"Just before morning dawned, while seeming to pass into a quiet sleep, thought I was standing upon a lone but beautiful highway. At my left was a vast plain, extending as far as the eye could reach, without a shrub or flower. On my right was a most beautiful grove; but not a leaf rustled, not the song of a bird was heard, to break the stillness. All was silent as though the great God had said, 'Be still!'

"For a moment I looked in wonder at the silent, lovely grove; then turned my eye to the plain, anxiously looking for some living, moving thing. Presently I discovered, far in the distance, an object approaching me, but could not discern what it was. As it drew nearer, the form of the cross was visible. O, how wonderful it appeared to me! Slowly and steadily it advanced; when suddenly my eyes beheld a suffering Savior, bearing the cross alone, in that lone place. As I gazed, he sank, in weariness and sorrow, to the ground. I made an effort to spring forward to help him bear the cross, but could not move. He arose, placing his eyes upon me. Such a look of love and sorrow combined, no language can portray. Advancing a few steps, with those speaking eyes still upon me, again he sank beneath his load. Again I tried to go to him, but was still powerless.

"Soon the scene changed. He arose with triumph. The victor's crown was upon his brow. His hair was white like wool, and no traces of sorrow were upon his face; but O, the look of love and tenderness! With outstretched hands, I sprang forward, saying, 'My Lord and my God! I will follow thee! I will obey thee; cheerfully will I bear the cross!' Our room seemed filled with Divinity, and a solemn, sacred awe pervaded the entire house. I saw such beauty and power in the cross as I had never known or thought of before; and all along my pilgrim-way, since that dear morning, I have loved the cross—loved to place myself upon it, and let it bear me!

"'The cross for Christ I'll cherish,
 Its crucifixion bear!'

"SPECIAL PRAYER BRINGS SPECIAL BLESSINGS.

"Two months later, months of precious toil for Jesus, sister Trauger came to me saying, with tears: 'I can not longer rest unless my niece is brought to Christ. What shall I do?' Prayer was proposed. I said, before kneeling, 'Let us see what God will say unto us!' Taking up my Bible, I opened to these words: 'Again I say unto you, that if two of you shall agree on earth as touching any thing that they shall ask, it shall be done for them of my Father which is in heaven!' Said I: 'Will you take this as the voice of God *now* speaking unto us? Will you claim the fulfillment of this promise?' She hesitated a moment; then, with streaming tears, said, 'I will!' We kneeled, and with the God-Man prevailed. During the week we waited patiently for the Lord. On Saturday, I awoke at an early hour with my whole heart panting after God, in desire for a fresh baptism of the Holy Spirit. So intense was the burden of soul that every breath seemed prayer. Just after breakfast, as husband was preparing to go to his quarterly-meeting, sister Trauger called and urged me to spend the Sabbath with her. I accompanied her to her quiet country home, and told her of my deep desire for a new plunge into the all-cleansing fountain.

"We retired to her consecrated room, to engage in devout prayer. Much of the day was spent in reading the Scriptures and in prayer. Sabbath morning dawned, and, with my soul still hungering for the bread of life and thirsting for the water of salvation, we prepared for church. Just before leaving the house, I again entered that room, my heart almost bursting under the burden, and, kneeling, opened the blessed Bible to these words: 'Behold, I will send my messenger, and he shall prepare the way before me; and the Lord whom ye seek shall suddenly come to his temple, even the messenger of the covenant, whom ye delight in; behold he shall come, saith the Lord of hosts.' Faith grasped the promise; and I arose as confident that the Lord would come to the temple of my heart as though the blessing were already given; then went up to the courts of the Lord's house, and tarried at class, calmly waiting for the coming of my Lord.

"Returning home with sister T. and her niece, for whom the special prayer was offered the previous Sabbath, passed the afternoon, prayerfully waiting, watching. The evening proved stormy, and we remained at home, improving the time reading the precious Guide. At nine, when we kneeled at the altar, my soul drew near to God. A little later, at my bedside, I bowed alone; but sister T. soon kneeled in silence by my side. After a few moments' pleading, the Lord, whom I sought, 'suddenly came to his temple, even the messenger of the covenant, in whom my soul did delight.' The whole night was passed in praise and adoration. The King of glory condescended to hold converse with a worm of the dust. My soul was satisfied, as with marrow and fatness. My mouth praised the Triune, with joyful lips. In the morning, I was invited to conduct family worship. The prayer led near the Throne.

> 'Heaven came down, our souls to greet,
> While glory crowned the mercy-seat.'

Sister T.'s niece, who was a professed Universalist, left the room in tears, saying to her aunt, who followed her into an adjoining room, 'O auntie! I would give all the world if I felt as Mrs. Crawford does this morning.'

"That evening, she was first at the altar, and there remained till her Universalism and sins were all washed away by the precious blood of Christ. 'If two of you shall agree on earth as touching any thing that they shall ask, it shall be done for them of my Father which is in heaven.' *Special requests bring special answers.*

"HEARS ANGELIC CHORISTERS.

"On the night in which occurred the death of my precious friend, Mrs. Mary E. Robinson, of Coldwater, and, as nearly as can be ascertained, at the same moment, I heard, as if in the air above our dwelling [parsonage, at Centerville], angel voices, sweetly singing, 'Homeward bound! homeward bound!' As the last strains died upon my ear, I repeated aloud, 'Home at last! home at last!' The music, together with the influence in my room, was wonderful, thrilling. Have ever believed that an indulgent Heavenly Father permitted me to hear the angelic choristers, as they bore away the pure spirit of my dear friend to her beautiful mansion.

> "'Let music cheer me last on earth,
> And greet me first in heaven.'"

March 10th Again at home. With trembling accent and blinding tears, said I to my dear friend, sister Crawford, as we were taking the parting hand, and speaking of the anticipated meeting with the loved ones at home, "You know there will be no dear companion to meet me at the depot with the 'welcome home,' as usual; and there will be the vacant chair, the vacant place at the table, and the vacant place as we kneel at the family altar." She replied, "I will pray that the joy of the Lord may go with you."

Homeward bound, 'mid the driving storm I changed cars at Albion; but was no sooner seated in the coach than the words came pressing themselves upon my mind: "Ye have not chosen me; but I have chosen you, and ordained you, that ye should go and bring forth fruit, and that your fruit should remain." "In my Father's house are many mansions: if it were not so I would have told you. I go to prepare a place for you."

As never before, I saw the blessedness of being thus chosen, as one of Christ's disciples, to go here and there proclaiming a risen Redeemer; and that I might forever rest in the assurance that my labor was not "in vain in the Lord;" that, however feeble the effort might appear to myself or others, however void of present results, yet the seed should spring up and produce fruit.

> "It may toss on many a billow,
> It may strand on many a shore.
> You may think it lost forever;
> But as sure as God is true,
> In this world or in the other,
> It shall come again to you."

And then, when these toils are all past, the last battle fought and the last victory won, in our Father's mansion above we'll rest. *There* no blinding tears shall ever come; "for the former things are passed away."

As these thoughts were occupying my mind, I glanced out of our coach window, and, as if hung from the windows of heaven by God's own hand, in front of the dark cloud overspreading the sky, and through the driving storm, I beheld the reflection of the lamps of our coach. And in some manner—how I can not tell, unless by the new arrangement now in our coaches of the Bible in the rack placed just under the lamps— was formed by shadow, just beyond the reflection of the lamps, a beautiful mansion encircled by a halo of light. And instead of thinking of the vacant places in the home-circle, the words of my dear M'Allister, "*I shall get my mansion first!*" brought to my mind a picture of our complete home-circle above, as we shall gather beyond the darkness and storms of this.

And I thought, If simply the reflection of earth-lights, and the shadow of God's blessed Word, can produce so beautiful a picture, and cause such joy to thrill the soul at thought of the home beyond the sky, what will it be to be there? For "eye hath not seen, nor ear heard, neither have entered into the heart of man, the things which God hath prepared for them that love him."

> "O, when shall I sweep through the gates?
>   The scenes of mortality o'er,
> What then for my spirit awaits?
>   Will they sing, on the glorified shore,
>   Welcome home? Welcome home?
>
> Yes: loved ones who knew me below,
>   Who learned the new song with me here,
> In chorus will hail me, I know,
>   And welcome me home with good cheer!
>   Welcome home! Welcome home!"

www.ingramcontent.com/pod-product-compliance
Lightning Source LLC
Chambersburg PA
CBHW031742230426
43669CB00007B/447